Paris

The Essential **Visitors'** Guide

Paris Mini Visitors' Guide
ISBN – 978-9948-03-448-3

Copyright © Explorer Group Ltd 2008
All rights reserved

All maps © Explorer Group Ltd 2008

Front cover photograph: Musée du Louvre – Victor Romero

Printed and bound by
Emirates Printing Press, Dubai, UAE

Explorer Publishing & Distribution
PO Box 34275, Dubai , United Arab Emirates
Phone (+971 4) 340 8805 **Fax** (+971 4) 340 8806
Email info@explorerpublishing.com
Web www.explorerpublishing.com

Introduction

Welcome to the Paris Mini Visitors' Guide. This mini marvel, perfect for visitors, was prepared by the same team that brought you the *Paris Complete Residents' Guide*. Written entirely by Paris locals, the book includes everything from the most interesting museums to the tastiest restaurants and swankiest bars. If you want to know more about Explorer Publishing, or tell us anything that we've missed, go to www.explorerpublishing.com.

Paris Mini Visitors' Guide

Editorial Team: David Quinn, Katie Drynan, Jenny Lyon, Grace Carnay
Contributing Editor: Sarina Lewis
Authors: Alicia Sheber, Amanda MacKenzie, Mira Lotfallah, Sarah Gilbert Fox, Sarina Lewis, Stephen Leonard
Photographers: Victor Romero, David Quinn, Maria Howell, Mark Ludbrook

Contents

Essentials

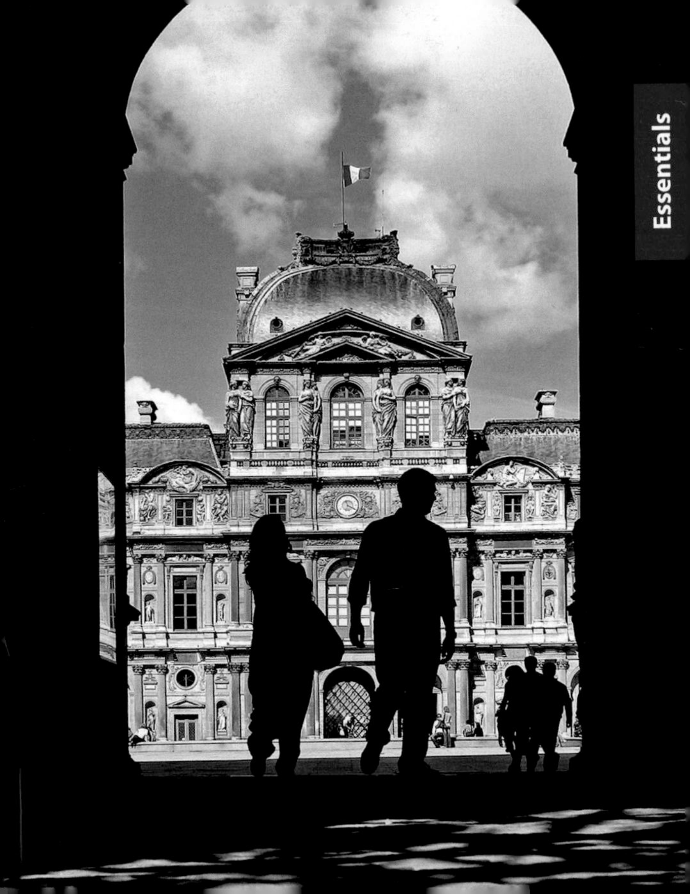

Bienvenue

City of romance, city of chic, city of light... Paris will bring you back on multiple visits, and each one will be just as special as the first.

Not content with having more than its fair share of postcard icons, Paris has the sort of random beauty that stops visitors in their tracks. You want culture? Count on an impressive array of world-class museums and cultural events, to which scarcely a season goes by without some new addition. Yet, for all it's activity, you'll still find Paris a touch less frenetic than other major world capitals. With its street corner carousels, open-air cafes and traditional markets, this is a city that has never quite shaken off its Old Europe pace. In short, it's a delight to explore.

Paris' historic heart beats between the Latin Quarter and the Marais. You won't have to look hard to find narrow streets and half-timbered houses dating back six centuries or more. Elsewhere, successive kings and emperors have left their stamp of grandeur. But it was Baron Eugene Haussmann who earned Paris its 'city of light' moniker after he established its first street lighting – and a lot more besides. As Prefect of the Seine, he flattened slums and mansions to make way for a mid 19th century vision of modernity. His new boulevards were lined with tall apartments, whose wrought iron balconies and restrained elegance provided a template for city construction long after Haussmann was gone.

A Notre Dame gargoyle

Hemmed in by its *Périphérique*, Paris might seem as though it's in danger of becoming a museum-city, but experienced close up, you'll find a different reality. New *quartiers* spring up out of wasteland, making inroads into greater Paris. As a city, Paris is constantly reinventing itself.

To grasp Paris as Parisians do, you should think of it in terms of the literary Left Bank and bourgeois Right Bank. For some visitors, that's a division that only works well when travelling downstream along the Seine. If you're one of them, don't despair, Paris is also a collection of villages. From genteel Passy to multi-ethnic Belleville, there's a sense of identity apparent to anyone prepared to explore.

When the time comes to venture out, hop on the metro, the bus, the tram or the train; public transport is extensive and great value. Often, though, travelling on foot is the most rewarding of all. Indeed, getting lost – as you certainly will – is all part of the fun.

Paris Checklist

01 Check Out The Champs

A massive revamp has put the oomph back into 'the world's most beautiful avenue.' Inhale the art nouveau elegance of Maison Guerlain, take in automotive art at L'Atelier Renault, or join the weekend strollers enjoying the Champs-Élysées' tree-lined vista. See p.70.

02 Head For The Heights

Notre Dame (p.78) isn't the only place to look down on Paris. Sample the captivating views from the Sacré Coeur (p.104) and the Eiffel Tower (p.114), take a lift to the top of the Arc de Triomphe (p.71) or blow away the cobwebs from the terrace of Galeries Lafayette (p.170).

03 Give In To Market Forces

Every *quartier* has a market, and each is different.
Shop against the grand backdrop of the Eiffel Tower
at the Marché de Saxe-Breteuil or head indoors to the
Marais' age-old Marché des Enfants Rouges. Rise early;
in most cases it's all over by lunchtime. See p.164.

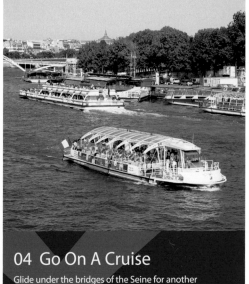

04 Go On A Cruise

Glide under the bridges of the Seine for another perspective on the city. Most cruises follow a circuit around the Île de la Cité and Île St-Louis, departing below the Eiffel Tower. For an interesting subterranean stretch, cruise along the leafy Canal St-Martin. See p.129.

05 Tour The Eiffel

The Iron Lady attracted criticism when it was built in 1889. Maupassant claimed to dine there because it was the only place he was spared the sight of it. Enjoy the shimmying night-time light show from anywhere in the city or up close at the Trocadéro. See p.114.

06 Get The Look

Create your own Parisian style courtesy of the city's fabulous boutiques. Or grab a bargain during *les soldes*, a twice-yearly affair. For inspiration check out the free weekly fashion shows at stores such as Galeries Lafayette and Printemps. See p.156.

07 Eat It Up

Welcome to France, where food takes second place only to God. Lounge in cafes, book in to a wine tasting lesson or course (p.146), or explore the wealth of wine bars, trad brasseries and haute cuisine restaurants for a real taste of the city. See p.176.

08 Get Physical

Cycling is a great way to explore. There are over 370km of cycle paths and with Vélib', the low-cost rental bike scheme (p.43), there's more incentive to get pedalling. History buffs and foodies can take a themed walking tour (p.135) to learn about local *quartiers*.

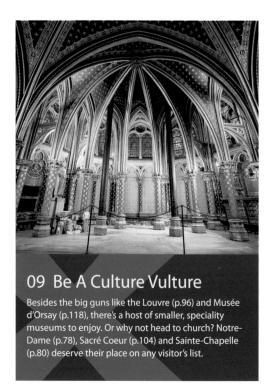

09 Be A Culture Vulture

Besides the big guns like the Louvre (p.96) and Musée d'Orsay (p.118), there's a host of smaller, speciality museums to enjoy. Or why not head to church? Notre-Dame (p.78), Sacré Coeur (p.104) and Sainte-Chapelle (p.80) deserve their place on any visitor's list.

10 Meander The Marais

The Marais (meaning 'marsh') enjoyed a glitzy interlude before slipping into centuries of neglect. Today, it's one of the most vibrant spots in Paris. Its boutique and bar-lined streets are just as lively on Sundays when other quartiers tend to doze. See p.62.

Best Of Paris

For Big Spenders

Cruise the Seine on a luxury yacht, champagne in hand (p.129); enjoy a bird's eye view of Paris by helicopter (p.133); be a VIP with a private tour guide (p.134); or shop with an in-the-know Parisienne (p.134) – Paris has a plethora of options for those looking to spend big. Fashionistas can exercise their gold card on the avenue Montaigne, place Vendôme and rue du Faubourg Saint-Honorè (p.160), where the world's biggest labels vend their glittery wares. The city's famed *grands magasins* (p.168) of Galeries Lafayette, Printemps and Le Bon Marché also attract fevered shoppers in droves. Or check in to any one of Paris' gilded hotels (think the Ritz, the Crillon or the George V) for a night to remember (p.49).

For Gourmands

The city of choice for many travelling gastronomes, Paris will not disappoint indulgent foodies. Take in one of the many food focused walking tours (p.135) to experience a broader view of the culinary landscape. Those that value the joy of independent discovery will find plenty on offer in the city's myriad of bars, brasseries and haute cuisine restaurants – simply choose an *arrondissement* and follow your nose. See p.176. Looking to get your hands dirty? Take up a cooking course (p.142) and enjoy shopping the markets before creating a meal to die for, or learn the finer arts of wine tasting in a Marais loft under the watchful eyes of a passionate professional (p.146).

For History Buffs

So much history, so little time. Get the inside info on Paris' notable museums (and the art within) with Paris Muse (p.133), an educational tour led by trained art historians. Those with decent French can discover the city's history in her lingua franca with the *Visites Conférences* organised by the Centre des Monuments Nationaux (p.133). Or uncover the stories of Montmartre, the French Revolution, or the second world war with Classic Walk's anecdote-filled adventures (p.135). Outside Paris, day-long *sorties* to the historic *châteaux* of Versailles, Vaux-le-Vicomte and Fontainebleau (p.127) provide plenty of intellectual fodder for the historically inclined.

For Lovers

With its stunning architecture, tree-lined boulevards, quiet courtyards and twinkling night-time vistas, Paris is a city built for love. If you seek simplicity, stroll along the Pont des Arts as the sun dips and the city's lights flicker alight, or take in an evening cycle of the city with Fat Tire Bike Tours (p.128) and revel in the romance. An aperitif with a view on floor 56 of Montparnasse tower or the newly renovated Jules Verne restaurant (p.246) atop the Eiffel Tower will set the mood, so too a dinner cruise along the Seine (p.129). Or visit lingerie specialist Sabbia Rosa (p.174) and be fitted for a handmade wisp of lacy lingerie to set pulses racing. In winter, wander the cobblestoned streets of the Île St-Louis (p.78) or the Marais (p.62) and let the whimsical atmosphere carry you away.

Visiting Paris

Situated in western Europe, and a major hub for international carriers, Paris is easily accessible. Start the adventure by train, plane or automobile.

Getting There

There are three airports serving metropolitan Paris: Aéroport Roissy-Charles de Gaulle (CDG) is France's main airport, smaller Orly Airport is 20 kilometres south of the city, and Beauvais, around 100 kilometres west of the city, which serves budget airline flights to European destinations. All major carriers fly direct to Paris, and most major cities can be reached direct. Air France is the national airline and flies to 185 destinations in 83 countries.

Most tickets are now electronic, and self-service check-in kiosks are in operation for many routes. Baggage allowances differ between airlines and classes of travel, so check with your operator when purchasing your ticket.

For visitors from other European cities, travelling to Paris by train can be just as quick as flying. France's Train à Grande Vitesse (TGV), or high-speed train, goes from Brussels to Gare du Nord (www.thalys.com) in less than an hour and a half, and the Eurostar service (www.eurostar.com) gets you from London to Paris in under three hours. The new TGV Est, travels from Strasbourg to Paris Gare de l'Est in two hours 20 minutes. TGV tickets can be purchased at any of Paris' six train stations, SNCF shops around town, or online at www.voyages-sncf.com.

Airlines

Aeroflot Russian Airlines	01 42 25 43 81	www.aeroflot.fr/eng
Air Canada	08 25 88 08 81	www.aircanada.com
Air China	01 42 66 16 58	www.us.fly-airchina.com
Air France	08 20 32 08 20	www.airfrance.fr
Air Tahiti Nui	08 25 02 42 02	www.airtahitinui.com
British Airways	08 25 82 54 00	www.britishairways.com
Cathay Pacific	01 41 43 75 75	www.cathaypacific.com
Continental Airlines	01 71 23 03 35	www.continental.com
Delta Airlines	08 11 64 00 05	www.delta.com
El Al Israel Airlines	01 40 20 90 90	www.elal.co.il
Emirates Airlines	01 53 05 35 35	www.emirates.com
Finnair	08 21 02 51 11	www.finnair.com
Iberia Airlines	08 25 80 09 65	www.iberia.com
Icelandair	01 44 51 60 51	www.icelandair.net
Japan Airlines	01 44 35 55 50	www.fr.jal.com
KLM	08 90 71 07 10	www.klm.com
Korean Air	01 42 97 30 80	www.koreanair.com
Lot Airlines	01 47 42 05 60	www.lot.com
Lufthansa	08 26 10 33 34	www.lufthansa.com
Northwest Airlines	08 90 71 07 10	www.nwa.com
PIA	01 56 59 22 60	www.piac.com.pk
Qantas	08 11 98 00 02	www.qantas.com.au
Singapore Airlines	08 21 23 03 80	www.singaporeair.com
Tap Airlines	08 20 31 93 20	www.flytap.fr
Thai Arlines	01 44 20 70 80	www.thaiair.com
United Airlines	08 10 72 72 72	www.united.com
US Airways	08 10 63 22 22	www.usairways.com

Essentials

Visiting Paris

From The Airport

Aéroport Roissy-Charles de Gaulle

Roissy   www.aeroportsdeparis.fr

CDG (or Roissy as it is sometimes called) is about 30 kilometres north-east of central Paris. Taxis cost between €34 and €60 depending on the traffic and *arrondissement*. There is a small surcharge for evenings and weekends and a supplement of around €1 for each piece of baggage which will be added on at the end of your journey. Taxis do not have child seats and credit cards are rarely accepted.

The bus is a cheaper option. The Air France Bus, or Les Cars, is an express shuttle running from the airport to various locations around Paris. See www.airfrance.fr for detailed scheduling and route information. Hours of operation are 05:45 to 23:00, with departures every 15 minutes, and travel time is about 45 minutes. A one-way ticket costs €12 for adults and €6 for children (ages 2-11); round-trip tickets are €18. Buses can be caught at Terminal 1, Terminal 2, and Terminal 2F. Shuttles from CDG to Orly also run from 06:00 to 22:30, with departures every 30 minutes, and travel time is about 50 minutes. A one-way ticket costs €16 for adults and €8 for children (ages 2-11).

The Roissybus is a special RATP service between CDG and rue Scribe, near the famous Opéra Garnier in the heart of Paris. Running between 06:00 and 23:00, the Roissybus departs every 15 minutes (or 20 minutes after 19:00), and the journey lasts between 45 and 60 minutes. A one-way fare costs €8.40.

L'Arc de Triomphe

CDG is also served by the RER B rail line. It runs from 05:00 to midnight, departing every 10 to 15 minutes on weekdays and takes around 25 minutes to the Gare du Nord train station, and 45 minutes to Denfert-Rochereau. A one-way fare is €8.00 for adults and €5.65 for children (ages 4-10). Both the bus and the train stop at all three terminals.

CDG also has its own TGV (high-speed train, see p.18) station with connections to various French and European cities. For schedules and fares, visit www.sncf.fr.

Orly Airport

Orly

01 49 75 15 15
www.aeroportsdeparis.fr

Taxis from Orly to the centre of Paris cost between €30 and €45, but are best avoided during morning and evening rush hours when long delays cause prices to escalate steeply. There is a supplement for baggage and credit cards are generally not accepted.

The Orlyval is an automatic metro which connects to the RER B rail line funnelling passengers directly in to Paris. There are seven stops on RER B within Paris and it takes about 35 minutes to reach the Châtelet Les Halles RER/metro in the 1st *arrondissement*. The service operates between 06:00 and 23:00, leaving every four to seven minutes from each Orly terminal (Orly Sud and Orly Ouest). Tickets for this service can be purchased in all metro and RER stations, and also at a special Orlyval sales desk in Orly airport. A one-way fare to the city centre is €9.05 for adults and €4.50 for children.

The Orlybus is more economical again, leaving from Orly Sud and Orly Ouest to the metro/RER station at Denfert-Rochereau with stops at Jourdan Tombe Issoire, Parc Montsouris and Alésia-René Coty (all in the 14th *arrondissement*). Hours of operation are 05:35 to 23:30, with departures every 15 to 20 minutes, and travel time is about 30 minutes. A one-way fare from the airport to Paris is €5.80.

The Air France Bus is an express shuttle which runs from Orly to the Gare Montparnasse and Invalides but will drop you off, if requested, at the Porte d'Orléans or Duroc metro stations. Hours of operation are 06:00 to 23:00, with departures every 15 minutes, and travel time is about 35 minutes. A one-way ticket costs €8 for adults, €4 for children (ages 2-11); round-trip tickets are €12. Groups of four or more benefit from a 15% discount. The bus departs from both terminals.

Beauvais

Beauvais

08 92 68 20 66

www.aeroportbeauvais.com

An official shuttle bus operates between Beauvais airport and Porte Maillot, 1 kilometre west of the Arc de Triomphe. The schedule is determined by flight arrivals and departures. Buses leave the airport around 20 minutes after flights arrive, while departing passengers travelling to the airport should be at Porte Maillot three hours and 15 minutes before their scheduled flight time. The journey takes an hour and a quarter, with a one-way ticket costing €13. Tickets can be bought online or from the bus driver at the time of departure. For further information, visit www.paris-beauvais.fr.

Visas & Customs

EU citizens can travel to Paris without the need for a visa. Citizens from countries such as Australia, the United States, Canada, New Zealand and South Africa are also permitted a three-month stay with no visa requirements. Citizens from some Asian and South American nations should check with their consular services. Customs laws restrict import of illegal goods, with limits also existing on cigarettes (200 per person), alcohol (one litre of spirits, two litres of wine), 50 grams of perfume, and cash. Importing of meat and dairy products is mostly forbidden.

Embassies & Consulates	
Australia	01 40 59 33 00
Austria	01 45 55 95 66
Belgium	01 43 80 61 00
Canada	01 44 43 29 00
Denmark	01 44 31 21 21
Finland	01 44 18 19 20
Germany	01 42 99 78 00
Greece	01 47 23 72 28
Ireland	01 45 00 20 87
Italy	01 45 44 38 90
The Netherlands	01 43 06 61 88
New Zealand	01 45 00 24 11
Norway	01 47 23 72 78
Portugal	01 47 27 35 29
South Africa	01 45 55 92 37
Spain	01 44 43 18 18
Sweden	01 44 18 88 00
Switzerland	01 49 55 67 00
United Kingdom	01 42 66 91 42
United States	01 43 12 22 22

Visitor Information

There are 10 official Paris welcome centres dotted across the city and the flagship office, the Pyramides centre, is just off l'Avenue de l'Opéra in the 1st. There you can find

The Louvre

Paris tourist information (museums, things to do, special events), make hotel reservations, book excursions and shows, and purchase 'Paris Visite' (transport) and museum passes.

The Pyramides centre near Opéra in the 1st is open every day from 09:00 to 19:00, between June and October; and from 10:00 to 19:00 Monday to Saturday, and 11:00 to 19:00 on Sundays, between November and May. Most other centres offer similar services. The Carrousel du Louvre centre, located in the inverted Louvre pyramid, offers information on the Île de France region. Visit http://en.parisinfo.com/our-welcome-centres for the locations of all the offices throughout Paris. The table opposite lists embassies and consulates in the city.

Local Knowledge

Climate

Paris enjoys four distinct seasons and some of the lowest rainfall in France. The climate is relatively temperate, although the winter can see temperatures of below freezing and summer temps can reach the high 30s. Autumn and spring – with their mild temperatures and beautiful colours – are perhaps the best seasons to visit. Annual rainfall is spaced fairly evenly throughout the year.

Crime & Safety

Paris is a relatively safe place, but with typical big city issues. Pick pocketing is rife so pay extra attention on the metro and in crowded public spaces. As a general rule, do not walk alone at night in the large metro transfer stations such as République, Châtelet-Les Halles or Montparnasse. The area around République is known for its drug trade, while Les Halles is populated by petty criminals and prostitutes. When taking the metro after dark sit in the first car. If an incident occurs, knock on the front window to alert the driver of the train.

Dos & Don'ts

With the large number of expats and international visitors, Parisian etiquette has loosened up over the past few years, but there still exists a few firm cultural taboos. Eating and drinking on the metro or in the street is frowned upon, neat attire should be worn when dining in restaurants (though those around the tourist centres are very relaxed), and it is polite to say *bonjour* and *au revoir* to shop assistants. On the roads, pay attention at pedestrian crossings.

Electricity

France has a 220 volt, 50 hertz electrical supply, with two-pin, round-hole sockets. For details and illustrations of the plugs used in France go to www.kropla.com/electric2.

In Emergency

French emergency teams are efficient, friendly and quick to respond. Only one problem: operators won't necessarily speak English. However, the number 112 can be called from any mobile phone and English-speaking operators are available. There are three main emergency response branches within France. The police, firemen (sapeurs-pompiers), who are often the first to arrive on the scene and who have medical training, and SAMU (Service d'Aide Médicale d'Urgence) deals with serious medical emergencies, providing ambulances and trained emergency response teams.

Emergency Numbers

English-Speaking European Emergency Number	112
Police (emergency)	17
SAMU (ambulance)	15
Sapeurs-pompiers (fire)	18
Lost Property	08 21 00 25 25
Lost/Stolen Credit Cards	08 92 70 57 05
24 Hour Pharmacy	01 45 62 02 41
Dental Emergency	01 43 37 51 00
Pediatric Emergency	01 44 09 84 85
SOS Help (English-language helpline)	01 46 21 46 46

Female Visitors

Women enjoy relative safety in Paris even when travelling alone, though there are a few points to consider. Travel in the first train car on the metro at night; the driver is just on the other side of the window in the front and can intervene or call for further assistance in case of harassment. Long metro transfer corridors such as Châtelet-Les Halles and Montparnasse should not be traversed alone at night. Les Halles, in the 1st arrondissement, is notoriously unsafe at night and should be avoided by men and women alike.

Language

French is the only official language. Many Parisians understand some degree of English, but a few French phrases will help you get by – see Basic French table opposite.

Lost & Found

Stolen items should be reported to the nearest police station immediately. For lost property call 08 21 00 25 25. For lost or stolen credit cards call 08 92 70 57 05.

Money

The currency is the euro. Banks are easy to find and most open Monday to Friday from 09:00 to 17:00, and many have Saturday hours. Some branches close for an hour during lunch. ATMs are similarly easy to locate. Connected mostly to banks or post offices, you will also find them at supermarkets and hotels. Many offer a choice of languages upon insertion of your card.

Basic French

Accidents & Emergencies

Accident	Accident
Ambulance	Ambulance
Doctor	Médecin
Driver's licence	Permis de conduire
Help!	Au secours !
Hospital	Hôpital
Insurance	L'assurance
Papers	Papiers, documents
Police	Police
Sorry	Je suis désolé

Introduction

My name is...	Je m'appelle...
What is your name?	Comment vous appelez-vous?

Taxi/Car Related

Airport	Aéroport
Hotel	Hôtel
Where is...?	Où est...?

Numbers

Zero	Zéro
One	Un
Two	Deux
Three	Trois
Four	Quatre
Five	Cinq
Six	Six
Seven	Sept
Eight	Huit
Nine	Neuf
Ten	Dix
Hundred	Cent
Thousand	Mille

Basic

Excuse me	Excusez-moi
Yes	Oui
No	Non
Pardon	Pardon
Please	S'il vous plaît
Thank You	Merci
You're Welcome	De rien

Greetings

Good morning/hello	Bonjour
How are you?	Ca va?
Fine, thank you	Bien, merci
Goodbye	Au revoir

Questions

How much is that?	C'est combien?
How?	Comment?
What?	Quoi?
When?	Quand?
Why?	Pourquoi?

For currency exchange (*bureaux de change*) there are several offices along the Champs-Élysées, as well as in other tourist areas, such as near Notre Dame Cathedral or L'Opéra. Commission rates vary, and some 'No Commission' places take a flat fee. Most bureaux de change are open from around 09:00 to 19:00. Larger hotels will also exchange money though the rates are not competitive.

Credit cards are widely accepted, though smaller neighbourhood stores often require a minimum purchase of around €10 to €15.

People With Disabilities

Paris is making strides to accommodate people with disabilities, though many buildings, pavements and metro stations remain a challenge for the wheelchair-bound. Restaurant toilets are often in the basement, and metro stations often don't have lifts. On the plus side, metro platform edges are marked with raised strips to warn the sight-impaired, and the city is installing audio indicators at traffic lights to ensure safe crossing.

Police

Paris' Préfecture de Police falls under direct jurisdiction of the Interior Ministry. With a ratio of nearly a thousand officers per arrondissement, armed police presence is evident in motorised vehicles, on horseback, by foot, bike and rollerblade. Police are recognisable in their dark blue uniforms and officers are usually approachable and ready to help someone in need.

Postal Services

La Poste boutiques can be found in each district, offering courier and regular mail services. A regular stamp costs 41 cents.

Public Toilets

Public toilets are few and far between, though there are some pay-operated, automated loos around popular tourist spots. Cafe and restaurant-owners frown upon the use of their facilities by non-clients, so make use of restrooms at every coffee stop.

Telephone & Internet

Telephone boxes are scattered at regular intervals along city streets, particularly around busier neighbourhoods. For these you will need to buy a *carte téléphonique*. These can be purchased from any neighbourhood *tabac*. Internet access is also plentiful, with most cafes now offering Wi-Fi access and wireless hotspots available at various parks and gardens.

Time

Paris is UTC+1 (previously GMT). *Tabacs* and cafes can be open as early as 08:00 along with *boulangeries* and news kiosks. Boutiques start later, opening from 10:00 and closing their doors at 19:00.

Tipping

Tipping is not a common custom in France. Leave a couple of euros for waiters, taxi drivers and hair stylists. In upscale restaurants and hotels, tipping is more frequent and generous. It is not usual to add a tip on a credit card payment.

Media & Further Reading

Newspapers & Magazines

Le Figaro, Le Monde, Le Parisien, and *Libération* are the top four French dailies, each selling for less than €2. English publications abound. *The International Herald Tribune,* costing €2, is edited and published in Paris, while international editions of newspapers such as *The Guardian* and the *Daily Mail* are also widely available.

Television

The majority of aired programs are in French, and international programmes are nearly always dubbed. Most hotels will offer a selection of international news and entertainment channels.

Radio

On the FM dial, Rire et Chansons (97.8) is a heavily commercial radio station, Radio Nova (101.9) plays hip-hop, world and electronic music, while Virgin Radio (103.9) is dedicated to the rock and pop genre. For jazz, tune in to TSF Radio du Jazz (90.4). At 105.9, France Info, part of Radio France, is the country's major news station broadcasting world news, in French, 24 hours a day. For an English language radio station try BBC World Service on 648AM.

Books

Paris attracts writers like Hollywood does actors, resulting in billions of pages about the city. Englishman Stephen Clarke's novel *A Year in the Merde* became a word-of-mouth bestseller in Paris a few years ago, and his latest, *Talk to the Snail*, is a non-fiction work serving up his humorous observations on the French. American journalist Adam Gopnik's *Paris to the Moon* is a compilation of his journal entries and *New Yorker* articles revealing an American family's love affair with the city. British novelist Polly Platt's book, *French or Foe* delves into the French culture and tells you how to ask directions without getting a snooty look. For factual information, Michelin's *Guide Rouge* is still the bible for French cuisine.

Websites

www.allocine.fr	Film show times
www.bonjourparis.com	Info and articles for expats
www.expatica.com	French news and expat guide
www.fusac.fr	Online small ads
www.maps.google.com	Searchable map site
www.meteo-paris.com	Paris weather
www.pagesjaunes.fr	Paris yellow pages
www.pap.fr	Property for sale and rent
www.paris.craigslist.org	Community classifieds
www.paris.fr	City of Paris official site
www.paris.org	Paris news and events
www.parisdailyphoto.com	Daily photo blog
www.parisinfo.com	Official tourist site
www.parisnotes.com	Useful info for expats
www.parisvoice.com	Webzine
www.ratp.fr	Metro and RER info
www.theparisblog.com	Expat blogs

Parisians love a great event. From street music and military parades to gourmet festivals and winter wonderlands, Paris has it covered.

Public Holidays

Five civil and six Catholic holidays dot the French calendar. Though France holds firm to the idea of separation of church and state, when it comes to vacation days the French prove to be quite devout. Alongside the traditional days of New Year's Day, Easter Monday and Christmas, the French also fete the end of the second world war (May's 1945 Victory Day) and their national holiday of Bastille (14 July), alongside the more saintly celebrations of Ascension (1 May) and Assumption (15 August).

Public Holidays	
New Year's Day	1 Jan
Labour Day	1 May
1945 Armistice Day	8 May
Bastille Day (La Fête Nationale)	Jul 14
Assumption	Aug 15
All Saints' Day	1 Nov
1918 Armistice Day	Nov 11
Christmas	Dec 25
Easter Monday	One day after Easter
Ascension Thursday	39 days after Easter
Pentecost Monday	50 days after Easter

Annual Events

Chinese New Year

13th Arrondissement

January or February

www.mfa.gov.cn/eng

Paris' Chinese community puts on an exciting show in welcoming the traditional Chinese New Year, occurring in January or early February. Parades and spectacles attract everyone to Chinatown in the 13th arrondissement.

Paris Fashion Week

Various Locations

February and July

www.modeaparis.com

Heavy hitters of the fashion world finish a whirlwind tour of international fashion capitals with a breathless haute couture showing in Paris. Over a few short days, industry experts display their wares and divulge the next great trends.

Salon d'Agriculture

Porte de Versailles

February/March

www.salon-agriculture.com

Former President Jacques Chirac rarely missed this popular agricultural convention held at Porte de Versailles every year. 'The largest farm in Europe' exhibits the finest specimens of cattle, swine and more in the great hall. Other halls offer tastings and lessons in green tourism.

Paris Marathon

Bois de Vincennes

April

www.parismarathon.com

Around 30,000 runners take part in the marathon, leaving a trail of paper cups and sweat behind them. The race attracts huge crowds, with an estimated 250,000 lining the streets.

Printemps des Musées

Various Locations

May

www.paris.fr

Piggybacking on the successes of La Fête de la Musique and Nuit Blanche is this fast-establishing tradition, which sees many museums stay open until 01:00 on one spring night with free admission to all.

Fête de la Musique

Various Locations

June

www.fetedelamusique.fr

Summer officially kicks off with a night of music unlike any other. Popular bands play on stages erected around town, while everyone with a guitar and a mic finds somewhere to jam. It's the only night of the year when the city suspends its sound restriction laws.

French Open

Roland Garros

June

www.rolandgarros.com

Paris welcomes the best tennis players in the world for the second Grand Slam event on the annual ATP tour, contested on the famed *terre battue* at Stade Roland Garros. Played out just to the west of the 16th arrondissement, the tournament is a source of Parisian pride and passion.

Summer Sales

Various Locations

June/July and January

Les soldes are a big deal in Paris, with the summer sales starting at the end of June and the winter sales at the end of January. Prices are continually marked down and great bargains are to be had in department stores and indie boutiques alike.

Top: Street performers. Bottom: Paris Plage

Essentials

Bastille Day

July

Champs-Élysées/Eiffel Tower   www.paris.fr

The national holiday, known in France as 14 Juillet, is celebrated with an impressive military parade down the Champs-Élysées and fireworks around the city at night.

Festival Paris Cinéma

July

Various Locations   www.pariscinema.org

In 20 cinemas and venues throughout Paris, this annual event draws cinephiles with its selection of 300 films, its star-studded guest list, and its low prices (€4 per film, or €20 for all you can watch).

La Chasse aux Trésors

July

Various Locations   www.tresorsdeparis.fr

The Paris Treasure Hunt debuted in 2006 and its 2007 sequel proved more popular. Several hunts take place in pre-determined *arrondissements*, so everyone can spend a few adventurous hours discovering or re-discovering a Parisian quarter while solving clues and interacting with local characters who hold the keys to the treasure.

Tour de France

July

Various Locations   www.letour.fr

Cycling's greatest race finishes on the Champs-Élysées, where spectators watch competitors complete eight laps before finishing at Place de la Concorde. This is an exciting and festive finale to the extraordinary three-week endurance event.

Paris Plage

The Seine

August
www.paris.fr

For those who can't escape August's heat, Paris brings the beach to them. Sunbathers stretch out along the sandy swathes of the Seine, umbrellas and lounge chairs included! Cool off under misting machines and stay at night for free weekend concerts.

Arènes de Montmartre

Montmartre

August/September
www.mysterebouffe.com

The three-week festival revives the popular Italian Commedia dell'Arte form of theatre in the open air of the historical Montmartre neighbourhood. Running from late August to the first week of September, the festival is put on by the Mystère Bouffe troupe.

Journées du Patrimoine

Various Locations

September
www.journeesdupatrimoine.culture.fr

Held on the third weekend of September, France's Heritage Days offer Parisians and tourists the opportunity to visit buildings and locales usually closed to the public. Around 12 million lovers of art and architecture take advantage of this special weekend each year.

Nuit Blanche

Various Locations

October
www.paris.fr

The first Saturday night in October never ends, with museums staying open extra late during this 'White Night'. Art exhibits of all kinds imaginable are on display into the wee hours and admission is often free.

Armistice Day

November

Arc de Triomphe   www.paris.fr

Recognising the end of the first world war and all soldiers who died in combat, the holiday is marked by a ceremonial wreath-laying at the Tomb of the Unknown Soldier under the Arc de Triomphe.

Salon du Chocolat

November

Porte de Versailles   www.chocoland.com

Strategically timed right around Halloween, this enormous chocolate convention attracts chocolatiers from around the world. Special shows and cooking exhibitions are staged throughout the event and free samples abound.

Christmas Season

December

Various Locations   www.paris.fr

December in Paris is a unique winter wonderland, with ice skating rinks open to the public at Montparnasse train station, on the first level of the Eiffel Tower and in front of the Hôtel de Ville. Be sure to witness the spectacular, festive window displays at department stores Printemps (p.171) and Galeries Lafayette (p.170).

New Year's Eve

December/January

Champs-Élysées   www.paris.fr

New Year's celebrations touch both sides of the calendar, kicking off with year-end parades and cultural events around Paris and the Île de France region.

La Grande Arche de la Défense

Getting Around

Paris is a city designed for walking. For those with weary feet though, one of the world's best public transportation systems is at hand.

Mayor Bertrand Delanoë has made it a mission to improve traffic circulation within the city. Recent years have seen an increase in bus and taxi-only lanes, allowing those vehicles smoother movement within Paris. Most recently Delanoë's Velib' bicycle rental scheme went into effect in July 2007 with thousands of bicycles available at hundreds of mini-stations around the city. As a visitor, forget hiring a car and make use of the extensive metro and bus routes which extend to every corner of the city.

Bus

Paris' RATP bus network is as extensive and efficient as its metro system. Lines generally run from 07:00 to 20:30, with limited Sunday service. From after midnight until 05:30, 42 'Noctilien' lines run throughout the city. A bus ticket costs €1.50. Tickets can be purchased individually on the bus (exact change not required), or you can buy a *carnet*, a pack of ten tickets which can be used on the metro, tram, RER or bus. Pass Navigo cards are the way to go if making multiple daily trips over a week or month. For bus routes and times, the little blue book *L'Indispensable* proves… indispensable. In addition, the RATP website (www.ratp.fr) contains an English-language tool.

Cycling

Traditionally not a popular form of transportation, bicycles recently made a huge entry onto the Parisian street scene thanks to the new Velib' scheme. Around 20,000 bicycles are available to the public for short-term rental at bike stations which can be found roughly every 300 metres. Short duration subscriptions – daily and weekly – can also be purchased at any station for €1 and €5, respectively. Regardless of which subscription you have, the first 30 minutes are free. You pay €1 for the first extra half-hour, then €2 for each half-hour after. With the short-term subscriptions these fees are deducted from your bank account. A few rules to remember: cyclists are not permitted to ride on pavements and must respect the right of way. The wearing of helmets is encouraged but not law.

Metro

With nearly 300 stations, the metro's 14 lines, along with its five express (RER) lines, serve 4.5 million people per day. Single-ride tickets are €1.50 and are also valid on buses and trams. A better deal is a *carnet*, 10 tickets for €11.10. In addition, monthly passes, known

Further Out

France's Train à Grande Vitesse (TGV), or high-speed trains, connect Paris to regional France and beyond. Tickets can be purchased at any of the six train stations in Paris, SNCF shops around the city, or online at www.voyages-sncf.com.

as Pass Navigo cards, afford unlimited trips within Paris for €53.50. Stations open at 05:30 and close at 01:00 except Saturday nights when they stay open an extra hour. Waits never extend beyond a few minutes at peak times. Digital clocks operate in most stations and indicate waiting times.

Rail

The five express lines of the RER serve as the city's deep underground rail system. With fewer stops than the metro system, this is a much faster way to travel with lines extending from the city centre to CDG and Orly airports and into the suburbs. RER times are posted on video screens and on poster boards in the stations. Make sure to look at the electronic boards on RER platforms indicating which stops the train will make to avoid heading off in the wrong direction or on an express train to a terminal way past your stop. Also, remember that RER lines require ticket verification upon entry *and* exit so keep your ticket until exiting the

Rent A Car

Renting cars in Paris, while not advised, is not too expensive. Three-day packages start as low as €33 a day with unlimited mileage. Weekly packages start at around €235 for a compact and €295 for a mid-size. Single day rates are around €50 for a compact and €60 for a mid-size. Book in advance from July to September, when car-less Parisians rent cars for their vacations.

station or you could be fined. Metro guards regularly patrol exit points, as well as the trains. The fine for not having a ticket is €25, payable on the spot.

Driving

As with the rest of continental Europe, people drive on the right side of the road. Compared to other major cities, Paris' streets are wide and its main conduits well-maintained. However driving is not for the fainthearted; streets are often congested, parking is difficult and expensive, and traffic police are constantly setting up random checkpoints and speed traps.

On city streets and multi-lane highways alike, passing another vehicle on the right is illegal. All passing must be done on the left. Speed limits within the city are marked by red and white circular signs reading either 30kph or 50kph.

Car Rental Agencies

Ada	08 25 16 91 69	www.ada.fr
Avis	08 20 05 05 05	www.avis.fr
Budget-Paripark	01 45 87 04 04	www.paripark.fr
Car'Go	08 25 16 17 16	www.cargo.fr
Europcar	08 25 35 83 58	www.europcar.fr
Hertz	08 00 25 10 00	www.hertz.fr
National/Citer	01 45 72 02 01	www.nationalciter.fr
Renault Rent	01 44 37 20 20	www.renaultparis.fr
Rent A Car	08 91 70 02 00	www.rentacar.fr
Sixt SAS	08 20 00 74 98	www.sixt.fr

(Some special cases may see 15kph.) On the *périphérique*, the maximum speed limit is 80kph. The maximum speed limit on French motorways is 130kph. Permanent radar cameras are set up along the *périphérique* and motorways to nab speeders, though signs indicate when you're nearing a radar camera, and websites offering directions, such as www.mappy.fr, always mark camera locations to help you out.

An important reminder regarding right of way; generally at intersections vehicles at the right have priority. This may seem logical, but keep in mind that Parisian streets do not have red stop signs.

Taxi

All taxis have white lights on their roofs. When the light is on, the taxi is available. Paris taxi drivers are a finicky lot; they will try and refuse less profitable trips, and don't like to take groups of four passengers, even if they technically can by charging a small supplement.

All taxis are metered. The meter should display €2 at the start of a trip and the minimum trip charge is €5.50. Count on paying a small supplementary fee after midnight.

From CDG airport, expect to pay around €40 to the city centre. From Orly it's a little over half that. Supplementary charges for baggage are minimal.

Taxis can be flagged down in the street or from taxi stands, which are marked by a post with a white light alongside footpaths. To call a taxi, dial 01 45 30 30 30. However, be aware: the meter runs from the moment they take your call.

Tram

The city's tram lines provide clean and quiet accompaniment to their big brothers, the metro, bus and RER. The newest to join the family, the T3 line along the city's southern rim, is the only tramway fully within the city limits. In the first six months of its existence the T3 carried five million passengers, and its popularity has spurred discussion on extending it eastward. Tickets operate the same as the other public transit systems – make sure to validate your ticket when you hop on board.

Walking

Paris was made to be enjoyed on foot, with nearly all main roads featuring wide, shaded pavements and clearly marked crossings. Famous bridges traversing the Seine are equally safe for pedestrians. Several are pedestrian-only, including the Pont des Arts and the Passerelle Simone de Beauvoir. Pay attention to drivers who don't obey traffic lights.

Water Taxi

Several years ago, the City of Paris formed a committee to discuss a mass transit system on the Seine. Nothing ever came of it. The closest thing Paris has is the Batobus, which is really only used by tourists. The Batobus (01 44 11 33 99, www.batobus.com) has eight stops between the Eiffel Tower and the Jardin des Plantes. Times differ throughout the year, with maximum hours from 10:00 to 21:00, May to September. There's no service in February. Day tickets cost €11, with two-day, monthly and season passes available.

Places To Stay

Whether you seek a cosy *chambre d'hôte* or palatial luxury, there's no wanting for choice when it comes time to lay your weary head.

Paris offers no shortage of lodging options, depending on budget, duration of stay and location. A few points to remember: in peak months lodging is tight; visitors should book early when planning trips in the months of June, September and October, when hotel occupancy rates are over 80%. On the flip side, bookings are a lot easier and less expensive in January and February. The hotel rating system runs from zero to four stars. Six top-range hotels have earned a rating above four stars and are known as '4 Luxe' hotels. In addition, some hotels fall outside the rating systems and call themselves 'Palace' hotels. Compared to other major cities, Paris' budget and mid-range rack rates are reasonable. A two-star hotel is €85 on average, while three-star hotels cost around €160 per night. At the luxury hotel level costs shoot up to €360 and above. All taxes are included within the price.

Bed and breakfasts, known as *chambres d'hôtes*, provide an inexpensive and pleasant alternative to hotels, though they do vary in quality and amenities. If you don't mind tight quarters or sharing a bathroom, the quaint charm and more personal touch may prove the perfect home base while in Paris. Visit www.goodmorningparis.fr for a selection throughout the city.

Four Seasons Hôtel George V

www.fourseasons.com/paris

01 49 52 70 00   From €735

Just off the Champs-Élysées, the George V offers elegant rooms, many with private terraces. Sophisticated restaurant Le Cinq has earned two Michelin stars. Make time to indulge at one of the city's finest spas.

Ⓜ Alma-Marceau, Map 3 E3 **1**

Hôtel Le Bellechasse

www.lebellechasse.com

01 45 50 22 31   From €200

This hotel has marked Christian Lacroix as the interior designer most in touch with today's *hôtel du charme* aesthetic. The 34 rooms each fall under one of seven designs, intended to reflect the *quartier*.

Ⓜ Solférino, Map 8 E3 **2**

Hôtel Caron de Beaumarchais

www.carondebeaumarchais.com

01 42 72 34 12   From €125

Owner Alain Bigeard has recreated 18th century *joie de vivre* in this sumptuous Marais hotel. The 19 rooms boast exposed-beams, Louis XIV-style wallpapers antique armoires, and chandeliers. Wi-Fi runs throughout. Ⓜ Hôtel de Ville, Map 10 B4 **3**

Hôtel de Crillon-Concorde

www.crillon.com

01 44 71 15 00   From €750

This is one of the most prestigious hotels in Paris with an incredible view over Place de la Concorde. Just minutes from the Champs-Élysées to the west and Jardin des Tuileries to the east, it offers 103 rooms, 39 suites, and five luxury apartments. Ⓜ Gare du Nord, Map 4 E4 ▪

Hôtel Duo

www.duoparis.com

01 42 72 72 22   From €115

This modern hotel mirrors the lively spirit and colour of the 4th. The staff are friendly and helpful, and the 39 rooms, including suites, are large for the price and location. Free Wi-Fi is available. There is also a small gym. Ⓜ Hôtel de Ville, Map 10 A3 ▪

Hôtel Fouquet's Barrière

www.fouquets-barriere.com

01 40 69 60 00   From €690

On the Champs-Élysées, this 107 room modern palace prides itself on its luxurious suites, interior garden and panoramic view of the city. There's a choice of bars and restaurants, and a luxury spa with a large indoor pool. Ⓜ Alma-Marceau, Map 3 E2 ▪

Hôtel Lutetia

www.lutetia-paris.com

08 00 05 00 11   From €300

This 230 room art deco-style hotel is minutes away from the Jardin du Luxembourg and St-Germain des Prés. The popular hotel bar is a favourite among local celebrities. There is also a gym.

Ⓜ Sèvres Babylone, Map 11 F1 **7**

Hôtel Plaza Athénée

www.plaza-athenee-paris.com

01 53 67 66 65   From €850

This hotel is on one of the most chic streets in Paris. Alain Ducasse oversees the cuisine in its five restaurants. The hotel's 188 rooms include 43 suites, and there's a well-equipped fitness centre and spa.

Ⓜ Alma-Marceau, Map 3 F4 **8**

Hôtel Thérèse

www.hoteltherese.com

01 42 96 10 01   From €150

The 43 rooms here have a four-star feel at three-star prices: think rich colours and materials, and large, luxury bathrooms. The spa around the corner offers hotel guests a free hammam with every massage booked. Ⓜ Pyramides, Map 5 B4 **9**

L'Hôtel

www.l-hotel.com

01 44 41 99 00   From €345

The name says it all, as if it was the only hotel in Paris. And for a long list of former lodgers, it was. Originally part of Queen Margot's palace, Oscar Wilde called it home. Dali and Sinatra have also graced its guest list. There's a small indoor pool. Ⓜ Saint-Germain-des-Prés, Map 9 B4 **10**

Pavillon de la Reine

www.pavillon-de-la-reine.com

01 40 29 19 19   From €370

Built by Henri IV in 1605, this elegant 56 room hotel overlooks the beautiful Place des Vosges. There's an attractive bar and lounge area. Breakfast on freshly baked breads from the boulangerie next door, then head out to explore the Marais. Ⓜ Bastille, Map 10 E4 **11**

Terrass Hôtel

www.terrass-hotel.com

01 46 06 72 85   From €260

This building dates from 1900 and offers 98 rooms, a cozy piano bar, and terrace dining with panoramic views over Paris. It's just minutes away from Sacré Coeur, the Moulin Rouge, art galleries, boutiques and restaurants. Ⓜ Place de Clichy, Map 2 B1 **12**

Hotel Apartments

For longer stays, fully furnished 'aparthotels' (01 40 03 67 52, www.appartcity.com) offer hotel service and apartment living conditions. However, many lack character and some are in shady areas. The Citadines chain is the best known, with 15 aparthotels spread throughout the city and a hotel-style rating system – the flagship one, Citadines Paris Opéra Vendôme, is comparable to a four-star hotel (08 25 33 33 32, www.citadines.com).

Another option made easy by the internet is direct-from-owner apartment rental. Minimum bookings of one week are usually required with costs sometimes breaking down to as little as €60 a night for a studio. Visit http://paris.craigslist.org, www.rentapart.com, and www.parisattitude.com for listings.

Hostels

There are four youth hostels in Paris belonging to the French branch of the International Youth Hostelling Network. Most rooms contain four to six beds with access to collective living areas. All ages are welcome but you need a membership card.

Hostels	
Cité des Sciences	01 48 43 24 11
Clichy	01 41 27 26 90
D'Artagnan	01 40 32 34 56
Jules Ferry	01 43 57 55 60

If you don't have one, you can purchase a 'Guest Card' onsite. The maximum stay limit is four nights due to the high demand. Visit www.fuaj.org for more information on locations and prices.

Exploring

Explore Paris

Paris defies the wisdom of a whole being greater than its parts. Explore any of its 20 *arrondissements*, and discover each area's unique flavour.

Spiralling outwards from the Louvre, the city unravels into separate *quartiers*, each as colourful and distinct as the last. Consider the warren-like lanes of Montmartre lined with bohemian boutiques and galleries; the grandeur of the premier arrondissement with its attention-grabbing landmarks (the Louvre and the place de la Concorde among them); and the bustling, scholarly Latin Quarter, home to the Sorbonne and ground zero for the city's student populace. For most visitors, the dilemma once they arrive in this city is where to begin.

History buffs will find plenty to entertain in the west of the city, around Trocadéro and les Invalides. Here, galleries and museums continue to pop up like wild mushrooms. It's worth noting here that museums and galleries are free on the first Sunday of the month, just get there early to beat the queues. As the cradle of Parisian civilisation the Île de la Cité and Île St-Louis offer plenty in the way of heritage sites, like the grand gothic architecture of the famed Notre-Dame. Nearby, the ancient, cobblestone streets of the Marais buzz with hip nightlife (it's also the city's premier gay district), an apparent irony given the *quartier's* history; first as a marsh and, second, as the central point for the city's Jewish community.

Visitors can also consider the dichotomy of a city split in two by the great waters of the river Seine: the Left Bank (*Rive Gauche*) encompassing St-Germain and the Latin Quarter is said to represent a more bohemian aesthetic, while the elegance of the Right Bank (*Rive Droite*) is set off by the luxe elegance of the place Vendôme, the Louvre and the commercial sophistication of *les grands magasins*.

Left, right, north, south... if all this sounds too much like an experiment in orienteering then book in to one of the many top-quality walking, bike or boat tours, designed to take the stress out of your stroll. Of course in a city where getting lost can prove half the fun, a wrong turn has the possibility of opening up a whole new view: as time marches on neighbourhoods continue to morph and shift – consider the *quartier* surrounding the Canal St-Martin, once derelict and forgotten, and now one of the centres for all things kitschy cool. Further out, certain sectors of the 13th are also experiencing a renaissance. And Parisian Mayor Bertrand Delanoë is keen the development should continue; not content with the successful launch of the Velib' project, which has seen thousands of bicycles available to the public on a rental basis around the city. Delanoë is also planning the set up of Autolib', whereby 2,000 cars will be put into communal play.

With so much on offer, it's hard to know where to start. This chapter takes on Paris by area, including a list of 'must-sees' alongside links to restaurants in the Going Out chapter (p.176) and boutiques in the Shopping chapter (p.158). In Further Out (p.124), the areas that are a little off the beaten track or that are worth a daytrip are all covered.

At A Glance

Looking for a particular museum, an art gallery or a park to picnic in? This handy reference will help you tick off all the important attractions.

Exploring

At A Glance

Beaches, Parks & Gardens

Sights & Attractions

Pont Royal and the Louvre

Beaubourg, The Marais & Bastille

Quirky and arty, this is where old school meets new. Discover Carnavalet's century-old relics and get up to speed with modern works at the Pompidou.

Love it or loathe it, the Centre Georges-Pompidou not only defines Beaubourg; for many Parisians, it is Beaubourg. Outside, a vibrant mood governs the plaza, a vast, sloping expanse where entertainers of all kinds come to strut their stuff. It's all good fun, but keep an eye on your wallet. Further south, the Marais is most visitors' idea of a perfect Paris stroll – cultured by day, hip by night. Largely spared the Haussmann treatment and neglected until recent decades, the area oozes history at every turn. Some magnificent mansions are now major museums, among them the Musées Picasso and Carnavalet. In Bastille, rue de Lappe and rue de la Roquette attract a trendy, young crowd with their fashionable restaurants, clubs and boutiques. Further north, seek out lively nights in Oberkampf. A short walk from place de la Bastille is the Canal St-Martin and its bohemian surrounds. For **restaurants and bars** in the area, see p.188. For **shopping**, see p.158.

Canal St-Martin

Stretching from the Square Frédérick Lemaître to the Rue Lafayette, this canal shortcuts a long loop in the River Seine on the eastern side of Paris in the 10th. The artificial waterway was opened in 1825 in order to supply Paris with water, following orders during Napoleon's rule. Today it serves a much more superficial purpose as a popular destination for Parisians and tourists who watch the barges navigate the series of locks and road bridges. The surrounding *arrondissement* is a revitalised, bohemian quarter with hip boutiques and a great nightlife. Ⓜ Goncourt, Map 6 D1 **33**

Galerie Karsten Greve
01 42 77 19 37

5 rue Debelleyme   www.artnet.com/kgreve-paris.html

With galleries in Cologne, Milan and St-Moritz, the Greve gallery is a big hitter, showing retrospectives from a variety of artists, such as Pierre Soulages, John Chamberlain and Jean Dubuffet. There's also a good play of 'young' talent, including Paco Knöller, Tony Cragg and Sally Mann. Open Tuesday to Saturday, 11:00 to 19:00. Ⓜ St-Sébastien Froissart, Map 10 D2 **34**

Galerie Marian Goodman
01 48 04 70 52

79 rue du Temple   www.mariangoodman.com

The Paris counterpart of this New York gallery is enviably housed in a Marais mansion. Its equally impressive programme includes work from Gerhard Richter, Steve McQueen, Chantal Akerman and Pierre Huyghe. Open Tuesday to Saturday from 11:00 to 19:00. Ⓜ Hôtel de Ville, Map 10 A3 **35**

Hôtel de Ville
01 42 76 40 40

Place de l'Hôtel de Ville   www.paris.fr

This city hall building is a 19th century replacement for the one that burnt down during the Commune in 1871. Its substantial exterior boasts some 136 sculptures of famous figures. The inside is just as fancy, with heavy chandeliers, copious gilding and wood panelling. At the spot where crowds once gathered to watch grisly public executions, Paris Plage now draws the masses in summer, along with the winter ice rink and an array of events in between. Excellent regular free exhibitions are held in the building. Tours, in French, English, and German are by appointment. Open Monday to Saturday, 10:00 to 19:00. Ⓜ Hôtel de Ville, Map 10 A4 36

Musée Carnavalet
01 44 59 58 58
23 rue de Sévignée
www.carnavalet.paris.fr

The Carnavalet is the principal museum on the history of Paris. Its collections fill two exceptional *hôtels particuliers*, one of which was the home of Madame de Sévigné, whose letters vividly capture courtly life under Louis XIV. Exhibits include rooms devoted to the Revolution and to the life and times of Madame de Sévigné; 18th century artisans' signs, and a wonderful intact art nouveau interior decorated by Alfred Mucha. You'll even find Proust's bedroom here and, of course, an extensive display of Napoleonic mementos. Children's workshops are offered. Entrance to the museum is free. Open Tuesday to Sunday 10:00 to 18:00. Ⓜ St-Paul, Map 10 D3 37

Musée Cognacq-Jay
01 40 27 07 21
8 rue Elzevir
www.paris.fr/musees/cognacq-jay

Not well-known but a charmer nonetheless, this Marais museum occupies a fine *hôtel particulier* dating back to the 16th century. The museum's focus, however, is the 18th century – the passion of its founder, Ernest Cognacq, who made his fortune from the former landmark department store, La Samaritaine. You'll see works by Greuze, Fragonard, Watteau and Boucher, along with Rembrandt and Joshua Reynolds, to name a few. Elegant Louis XV furniture, Meissen porcelain and other decorative objects from the era also have pride of place. Open Tuesday to Sunday 10:00 to 18:00. Closed on public holidays. Ⓜ St-Paul, Map 10 D3 🔢

Musée des Arts et Métiers
60 rue Réaumur

01 53 01 82 00
www.arts-et-metiers.net

This museum gets off to a flying start with its wonderful setting. Within the ancient priory of St-Martin-des-Champs, it pays homage to technology from the 16th century onwards.

Among the flying machines on show is an extraordinary feathered number which, unsurprisingly, never got airborne. You'll also find cars, early bikes and Lavoisier's laboratory from the 18th century, along with all manner of other inventions. On certain days, the museum opens up its gallery of exquisite early automatons and you can see them in action (kids are generally spellbound). For refreshments, there's a sleek, modern cafe. Open Tuesday to Sunday from 10:00 to 18:00 (Thursday until 21:30). Ⓜ Réaumur–Sébastopol, Map 6 B4 **39**

Musée National d'Art Moderne
01 44 78 12 33
Place George Pompidou
www.centrepompidou.fr

Focusing mainly on art produced between 1905 and 1950, this major art collection takes up the whole of the fourth and fifth floor of the Pompidou Centre. Among the 58,000 paintings, sculptures and other media are works by Picasso, Matisse and Warhol. Only a selection of the collection is displayed at any given time, and works are regularly changed to keep perspectives fresh. The Centre's book and gift shop is a good source of gift inspiration, and you can grab a snack at the Café Mezzanine. One floor up from the museum, Georges restaurant offers an impressive panorama. Tickets can be purchased on the ground floor. Open daily (except Tuesdays) from 11:00 to 21:00. Closed 1 May. Ⓜ Hôtel de Ville, Map 10 A2 **40**

Musée Picasso
01 42 71 25 21
5 rue de Thorigny
www.musee-picasso.fr

Behind its neoclassical facade, this 17th century *hôtel particulier* houses the most extensive collection of Pablo

Picasso's works in existence, including paintings, engravings, ceramics and sculpture. Arranged chronologically, they cover the main periods of a staggeringly prolific artistic life. The mansion itself is a delight, with its ornate walls and magnificent staircase. Entry is free for under 18s and on the first Sunday of the month. Open Tuesday to Sunday: April to September, from 09:30 to 18:00; October to March from 09:30 to 17:30. Ⓜ St-Sébastien Froissart, Map 10 D3 **41**

Place des Vosges

The oldest square in Paris, the Place des Vosges was built by Henri IV from 1605 to 1612. A true square (140m x 140m), it embodied the first European programme of royal city planning, the prototype for all the residential squares of European cities to come. Today it is a popular haunt come Sundays when the restaurants lining the square spread out their tables onto the edges of the linden-lined square.

Ⓜ St-Paul, Map 10 E4 **42**

St-Eustache
Place René Cassin

01 42 36 31 05
www.saint-eustache.org

Work on this imposing church was begun in 1532 but took over a century to complete; the result is Gothic architecture with Renaissance trappings. Among the highlights are the elaborate tomb of Colbert, fine stained glass windows and a naive sculpture added in the 1960s to reflect the great market trading era of Les Halles. Great acoustics with an organ to match make this a popular place for recitals. Open daily from 09:00 to 19:30. Ⓜ Les Halles, Map 9 E1 **43**

If you only do one thing in...
Beaubourg, The Marais & Bastille

Explore Musée Carnavalet (p.64). Its recreations of times past are extraordinary.

Best for...

Drinking: Indulge in an aperitif at chic restaurant Le George (p.191) in the Centre Georges-Pompidou.

Eating: Dine at Guillaume (p.192), where chef Xavier Thierry's delectable cuisine is served upon his aunt's tables, beneath his mother's artwork.

Culture: Explore the Viaduc des Arts (www.viaduc-des-arts.com), a community of around 50 artists and craftsmen housed beneath old railway arches.

Outdoor: Take in the gardens of the *promenade plantée*, a strip of green oasis floating above the Viaduc des Arts (www.viaduc-des-arts.com).

Shopping: Head to rue des Francs Bourgeois (map 10 B3) where the fashion-conscious locals shop.

The Champs-Élysées

Oh the Champs-Élysées. Stroll along the tree-lined avenue and take in some of the city's premier sights; it's the perfect place to start exploring.

The 'world's most beautiful avenue' runs nearly 1.2 miles between Étoile and the place de la Concorde. It traces the old Royal Axis which once led west to the royal residence at St-Germain-en-Laye. After more than a decade in the doldrums, the Champs-Élysées has largely regained its lustre, thanks to a major facelift and tougher regulations. The western end is marked by the unmistakable L'Arc de Triomphe. At the eastern end is place de la Concorde. This octagonal square, the city's biggest, has a bloody history; some 1,300 souls, including Louis XVI and Marie-Antoinette, were guillotined here during the Terror of 1794, before being unceremoniously buried near rue Pasquier.

Highlights of a Champs stroll include peeking into the lavish art nouveau interior at Guerlain's perfume boutique (p.175), nibbling macaroons within Ladurée's elegant tearoom (p.171), and checking out the Grand Palais (p.72) and the Petit Palais (p.74) on either side of nearby avenue Winston Churchill before taking a stroll across the gilded bridge, Alexandre III. It's worth stopping for a (pricey) cocktail or a coffee in one of the many cafes lining the avenue as it's a nice place to sit and people watch. For restaurants and bars in the area see Going Out on p.200. For shopping see p.175.

L'Arc de Triomphe

L'Arc de Triomphe

Place Charles de Gaulle

01 55 37 73 77
www.monum.fr

The Arc de Triomphe holds a special place in Parisian hearts. Rising out of a swirling sea of traffic, this is a suitably grand monument to the victories of France's greatest military genius, even if Napoleon didn't live long enough to see its completion. It now harbours the *Tomb of the Unknown Soldier*, honouring the dead of the first world war. Alongside the inscribed names of battles and generals, there are bas-reliefs all around its surface (the eye-catcher is Rude's impassioned *Le Départ des Volontaires*, better known as *La Marseillaise*). Ascend the monument to appreciate a perspective that runs from the Champs-Élysées to the Louvre, then turn around for a peek at La Grande Arche de la Défense. The Arc

de Triomphe is pivotal to the city's calendar of pomp and ceremony, it is the dramatic backdrop for the Presidential parade every 14 July and other mass draws such as the Tour de France cycling race. Open daily: April to September, from 10:00 to 23:00; October to March, from 10:00 to 22:30. The monument is closed on public holidays.

Ⓜ Charles de Gaulle Étoile, Map 3 C1 ❶

Chapelle Expiatoire

01 44 32 18 00

29 rue Pasquier

www.monuments-nationaux.fr

Partly hidden by trees, this grand but rather lonely chapel in the shape of a Greek cross was commissioned by Louis XVIII in 1826. It stands on the ground where the remains of his brother, Louis XVI and Marie-Antoinette were hastily buried (an ignominy they shared with 3,000 other guillotine victims, including many in the Revolutionary government). The bodies of the king and queen were removed and placed in the Basilique St-Denis. The chapel contains Jean-Pierre Cortot's sculpture of Marie-Antoinette *Succoured By Religion*, while, below, a black and white marble altar marks the spot where both royal bodies were found. There's a small admission fee. Guided tours are available on reservation. Open Thursday to Saturday 13:00 to 17:00. Closed on major public holidays. Ⓜ St-Augustin, Map 4 E1 ❷

Grand Palais

08 92 68 46 92

Avenue Winston Churchill

www.grandpalais.fr

Built for the 1900 Universelle Exposition, this extravagant palace half way down the Champs-Élysées was conceived

Grand Palais

as a monument 'to the glory of French Art.' It's managed by the national museums authority and, taken as a whole, its galleries now constitute France's most important venue for international exhibitions. The fabulous glass hall reopened in 2005 after renovation and now hosts, among other things, the annual FIAC art fair. Pre-booking is advised at all times; for visits before 13:00, it's obligatory. Open Monday, Thursday and Sunday from 10:00 to 20:00; Wednesday from 10:00 to 22:00. Ⓜ Champs-Élysées – Clemenceau, Map 4 B4 🖹

Jardin des Champs-Élysées

Between the Rond-point des Champs-Élysées and the Place de la Concorde you will find the Jardins des Champs-Élysées, a quiet green space of rolling lawns planted with flower beds and criss-crossed by countless paths. Designed in the 19th

century to represent an English-style garden, it was restored and embellished in 1994. Highlights include the restaurant Le Pavillon de l'Élysées and théâtre Marigny. Also worth a look is the elegant entrance to the Palais de l'Élysée, home to the French President. Ⓜ Franklin D. Roosevelt, Map 4 C3 🔢

Musée Jacquemart-André

158 blvd Haussmann

01 45 62 11 59
www.musee-jacquemart-andre.com

Not just a fabulous art collection (it's brimming with works of the Italian, Dutch and French masters), the museum offers a fascinating window into the life of the upper crust during the 19th century. Built to accommodate their treasures, this was the home of banking heir Edouard André and his wife, the artist Nélie Jacquemart. A double spiral staircase leads the way to their 'Italian Museum', where André indulged his taste for Florentine masterpieces by Uccello, Botticelli and Perugini. There are free audioguides, a well-stocked shop and Tiepolo gracing the tearoom ceiling. Open daily from 10:00 to 18:00, including public holidays. Ⓜ St-Augustin, Map 1 C2

Musée de Petit Palais

Ave Winston Churchill

01 53 43 40 00
www.petitpalais.paris.fr

Small (smaller than the Louvre, at least) and perfectly formed, this is the Ville de Paris' own collection of art treasures, which ranges from early Greek sculptures to late 19th century art. Exhibits include some fine art nouveau pieces and a works by Cézanne, Renoir and Bonnard. With its many mosaics and Belle Époque flourishes, the 1900 building is delectable. Round off your visit at the modern cafe overlooking the garden. There's a well-stocked book and gift shop within the museum. Entry to the permanent collection is free. Open Tuesday to Sunday 10:00 to 18:00.

Ⓜ Champs-Élysées – Clemenceau, Map 4 C3 🟥

Palais de la Découverte

Ave Franklin D. Roosevelt

01 56 42 20 21
www.palais-decouverte.fr

While it can't really compete with the newer science museum at La Villette, the Palais works hard to infuse fun into learning about science – and, for the most part, it does a good job. Demos and workshops range from static electricity to chemistry in the art of chocolate-making, and there are good sections on biology and geoscience, along with some excellent temporary shows. Children's activities are on offer, though most are aimed at French speakers. The planetarium remains the star asset. Open Tuesday to Saturday 09:30 to 18:00; Sunday and public holidays 10:00 to 19:00.

Ⓜ Champs-Élysées – Clemenceau, Map 4 A3 🟥

Pinacothèque de Paris

28, place de la Madeleine

01 42 68 02 01
www.pinacotheque.com

This enormous, private museum recently opened in the prestigious 8th *arrondissement*. Art historian Marc Restillini's mission breaks away from the more traditional and didactic approach to art adopted at the likes of the Musée d'Orsay – to attract a new audience for modern and contemporary creation. So far things auger well, with a grand Roy Lichtenstein retrospective for openers. Open daily 10:30 to 18:30. Ⓜ Madeleine, Map 4 E2 🟥

If you only do one thing on...
The Champs-Élysées

Simply start at one end and walk the length of it, stopping for a coffee or cocktail as you go.

Best for...

Eating: Join the hordes lining up to taste the delectable treats in the tearoom of Ladurée (p.171), where macaroons are a speciality.

Drinking: The three-storey Culture Bière (at number 65) is a sophisticated spot in which to quench a rabid thirst.

Sightseeing: Take the elevator to the top of L'Arc de Triomphe and enjoy a bird's-eye view of the bustling boulevard.

Shopping: Duck into Le 66 (at number 66), a newly opened trendy store that will tell you all you need to know about the state of French fashion.

Families: There's plenty to entertain at the new Citroën showroom (at number 38), the first new building here in more than 30 years.

Île de la Cité & Île St-Louis

Almost a world apart from the rest of the city, these bite-sized islands, located right in the centre, exude an old-world charm and decadence.

The Île de la Cité is the cradle of Paris, the island settled by the Celtic Parisii and the town the Romans knew as Lutetia. Haussmann's 19th century clean-up operation was radical, but it had the effect of focussing the spotlight on two major landmarks: La Conciergerie and Notre-Dame. The island's other must-see attraction is La Sainte-Chapelle, whose delicate spire soars above its immediate surroundings. To get a good sense of the island, an attractive approach is the Pont Neuf. In 1607, it was a novelty, the first bridge to be furnished with pavements where pedestrians could escape a splattering from muddy carriage wheels. It's now the city's oldest bridge. On the Île St-Louis browse the snug antique shops and galleries. The island was swampy and vagabond-ridden until the 17th century, when the speculator Christophe Marie transformed it with the *hôtels particuliers* that are now coveted real estate. *For restaurants and bars in the area, see p.208. For shopping, see p.163.*

Cathédrale Notre-Dame de Paris

01 42 34 56 10

Place du Parvis Notre-Dame   www.cathedraledeparis.com

Built between 1160 and 1345, this Gothic masterpiece turned Paris into an ecclesiastical capital. Hard times came though, notably when Revolutionary zealots decapitated its carved Old Testament kings and made it a temple to the Cult of Reason, in which secularism and atheism was the rule of the day. Even Napoleon's coronation here couldn't stop its decline in the 19th century; it took Victor Hugo and the Gothic Revival architect Viollet-le-Duc to do that. The twin towers, rose window and triple doorways of the west front are a triumph of harmony. Inside, the soaring knave is flanked by 37 chapels containing *The Mays* – paintings by Charles Le Brun and other artists which were donated by wealthy guilds. On Sunday afternoons, organ recitals are free. The Treasury houses ornate vestments and plates. The crown of thorns can be seen annually on Good Friday. Complete your visit by climbing the towers; tickets are sold by the north tower. The cathedral is open weekdays from 08:00 to 18:45 and Saturday and Sunday from 08:00 to 19:15. Ⓜ Cité, Map 12 F1 🅑

La Conciergerie

1 Quai de l'Horloge

01 53 73 78 50
www.monum.fr

Despite its forbidding aspect, the Conciergerie wasn't always a prison (though one conical tower housed a torture chamber). It takes its name from the 'concierge' ('King's steward') left in place by Charles V when he moved the royal residence. Its most infamous period was under the Tribunal Révolutionnaire, when more than 2,700 condemned prisoners spent their last days here; Marie-Antoinette being the most famous. After making their way through the immense 14th century vaulted hall (the oldest of its kind in Europe) and the bookshop, visitors can peer into her cell. It's a reconstitution, but – guarded, cramped and comfortless – it's no less poignant for that. If you intend visiting the Sainte-Chapelle, plump for a combined ticket. Open daily: March to October, 09:30 to 18:00; November to February, 09:00 to 17:00. Ⓜ Cité, Map 9 E4 🄸

La Crypte Archéologique
1 place du Parvis Notre-Dame
01 55 42 50 10

Most of medieval Île de la Cité was lost under Haussmann's redevelopment of the city, but vestiges of shops and streets have been preserved below ground on the plaza in front of Notre-Dame. You'll also find some sections of quayside and rampart that date back to the Roman city of Lutecia (Lutèce in French), together with an 18th century orphanage and 19th century sewer. While the resulting hotch-potch can be a little difficult to make sense of, the models of the settlement's development are more enlightening. Open Tuesday to Sunday 10:00 to 18:00. Ⓜ Cité, Map 12 F1 🄸🄾

La Sainte-Chapelle
Blvd du Palais
01 53 40 60 97
www.monuments-nationaux.fr

The Sainte-Chapelle was built between 1242 and 1248 as a shrine for the crown of thorns and a fragment of the true cross which Louis IX – later St Louis – purchased at huge cost from Byzantium (they're now under lock and key at Notre-Dame). Despite being enclosed by the Palais de Justice, it remains one of the city's jewels. The lower chapel's rich blue, starred ceiling was built to accommodate the prayers of servants. The upper chapel for king and court achieves an almost mystical effect, thanks to the 15 metre-high stained glass windows that bathe the space in colour. Remarkably, two-thirds of them are original and they depict almost the entire bible. The delicate spire you can see outside dates from 1853. A combined ticket includes access to La Conciergerie close by. Open daily: March to October, 09:30 to18:00; November to February, 09:00 to 17:00. Closed 1 January, 1 May and 25 December. Ⓜ Cité, Map 9 E4 **11**

Marché aux Fleurs
Place Louis-Lépine
Surviving since the early 19th century is the permanent Marché aux Fleurs, arguably the largest and most beautiful flower market in Paris. Make a weekend visit and watch all of Paris descend to pick up the greenery that will brighten the wrought-iron railings on apartment balconies across the city. On Sundays the market also sells caged birds and small pets. Open daily from dawn till dusk. Ⓜ Cité, Map 9 E4 **12**

Towers of Notre-Dame de Paris   01 5 31 07 00
Place du Parvis Notre-Dame   www.monuments-nationaux.fr
The design of the towers of Notre-Dame allow for a limited number of visitors, but your patience is well rewarded. You'll share the amazing views with the baleful gargoyles added by Viollet-le-Duc in the 19th century. In July and August the towers stay open into the evening, and they are free on the first Sunday of the month. Open daily: April to September, 10:00 to 18:30; October to March, 10:00 to 17:30. The towers are closed on major public holidays. Ⓜ Cité, Map 12 F1 **13**

If you only do one thing in...

Île de la Cité & Île St-Louis

Duck into Notre Dame (p.78) and marvel at its gothic gargoyles and lofty spires.

Best for...

Eating: Skip the pricey cafes and crêperies and head for Mon Vieil Ami (9 place de la Madeleine) for modern takes on old French favourites.

Drinking: The quirky tearoom of La Charlotte de l'Île (p.163) is a hidden treasure, serving up delectable treats.

Culture: La Sainte-Chapelle's (p.80) stained glass windows are breathtaking. Combined with tickets for a classical music concert, it's unforgettable.

Families: Visit the small bridge connecting the two islands for free live entertainment at weekends.

Outdoor: Beautiful gardens behind Notre-Dame provide prime views of the historical church.

Clockwise from top: Detail of ceiling in Notre Dame, Interior of Notre Dame, La Conciergerie

The Latin Quarter

Studenty at heart, this *quartier's* cobbled streets have a bohemian vibe. Visit gothic churches or pay your respects to the literary greats.

Latin is no longer the lingua franca of Sorbonne students, nor will you find many chain-smoking intellects in the cafes of Boulevard St-Michel, but the lively, narrow streets of the Latin quarter are still irresistible for strolling and people-watching. The area is steeped in history. The Église St-Séverin is a jewel with sinuous carved pillars and vaults, the 13th century Sorbonne University is here, not to mention the Panthéon, commissioned by Louis XV as a basilica to Sainte-Geneviève (the teenage Gallo-Roman queen who worked wonders with Parisians' morale when Attila the Hun's armies menaced the city). At the corner of boulevards St-Germain and St-Michel, you can escape the bustle in the medieval gardens of the Musée National du Moyen Age. In a splendid double-act, they're laid around the walls of the ancient Roman baths. *For **restaurants and bars** in the area, see p.208. For **shopping**, see p.164.*

Arènes de Lutèce

47 rue Monge www.paris.fr

Although the first to second century arena is one of two important vestiges of the Roman city of Lutetia, there's every chance you'll have it pretty much to yourself – that is, unless

Grande Galerie de l'Évolution, Jardin des Plantes

the locals have turned up to play *pétanque* or five-a-side. In its day, thousands gathered here to watch gladiators draw blood or the latest dramatic offering. Some of the terraced seats have survived intact. The vestiges of the arena were buried here for centuries until the construction of rue Monge brought them to light. Open daily: summer, 08:00 to 22:00; winter, 08:00 to 17:30. Ⓜ Place Monge, Map 15 D1 **14**

Jardin des Plantes

57 rue Cuvier

01 40 79 54 79

www.mnhn.fr

The city's main botanical gardens started life as a royal medicinal garden in 1635. Encompassing the Grande Galerie de l'Évolution and its neighbours, a small zoo and several cafes, it will easily swallow up an afternoon's visit. Although the hothouses and other elements are gradually being renovated, the gardens are lovely to wander through, with

avenues of Russian plane trees, alpine and kitchen sections and carp-filled ponds planted with exotic plants. Local joggers have adopted the labyrinth for its shady uphill paths, and the expansive lawn is a great place to sunbathe and enjoy the grandiose vista. Entrance to the main garden is free; but there's a fee for other attractions. Open daily: winter, 08:00 to 17:30; summer, 08:00 to 20:00. Ⓜ Jussieu, Map 15 F1 15

Jardin du Luxembourg
www.paris.fr

In the heart of the Latin quarter, this civilised and lively park has wide appeal, attracting large summer crowds especially around the baroque Fontaine des Médicis, where chairs are quickly snapped up. The park and the Palais owe their existence to Marie de Médicis, who sought to recreate the flavour of her native Florence. (The palace now encompasses the seat of the French Senate while temporary exhibitions are held at the Musée de Luxembourg). Chess-players gather under the trees, children can rent dinky boats to launch on the grand basin, there are tennis courts, a boules terrain and an apiary. Already rich in statues, the park also regularly hosts contemporary art exhibitions. Open daily from 07:30 to dusk in summer; 08:00 to dusk in winter.

Ⓜ Luxembourg, Map 12 B4 16

La Mosquée de Paris   01 45 35 97 33
39 rue Geoffroy St-Hilaire   www.mosquee-de-paris.org

Paris' main mosque, a dazzling white Hispano-Moorish inspired structure with a green-tiled minaret, was built in the 1920s. It's the spiritual centre of the country's mainly Algerian Islamic community. There's a small admission charge to visit the outer courtyard and library, either under your own steam or with a guide. Within the complex, there's also a pleasant cafe that serves mint tea on brass trays, a traditional hammam, and a polychrome restaurant. Open daily except Friday, from 09:00 to 12:00 and 14:00 to 18:00. Closed on religious holidays.

Ⓜ Place Monge, Map 15 E2 🔢

Le Panthéon
Place du Panthéon

01 44 32 18 00
www.monum.fr

Soufflot's neoclassical masterpiece used to dominate the skyline of Paris from its lofty position on the Montagne Sainte-Geneviève. It's still the Latin quarter's most notable monument. Conceived as a church, it was no sooner completed than the Revolutionary authorities turned it into a necropolis for great men (though not all of those honoured got to stay). It fluctuated between secular and religious use until the 1880s. With its grandiose stone tableaux and painted friezes (some are by Puvis de Chavannes), the choir makes you feel small and, if that isn't enough, a replica of Foucault's Pendulum, suspended from 67 metres up, demonstrates that the planet is relentlessly revolving. At rest in the well-lit crypt are Voltaire, Rousseau, Hugo, Pierre and Marie Curie and Jean Moulin. On fine days, it's worth paying a little extra to climb the dome for great views. Open daily: April to September, from 10:00 to 18:30; October to March, from 10:00 to 18:00.

Ⓜ Cardinal Lemoine, Map 12 E4 🔢

L'Institut du Monde Arabe

01 40 51 38 38

Rue de Fossés St-Bernard

www.imarabe.org

The Institut was designed by Jean Nouvel, one of the darlings of the architectural scene, who has since furnished Paris with the Fondation Cartier and the Quai Branly museum (p.119). His walls of light-adjusting steel and glass apertures are reminiscent of Moorish latticed screens, and the result still cuts quite a dash by the Pont de Sully. The museum on the seventh floor displays Middle Eastern art and scientific treasures, amply revealing the pioneering influence of eastern scientists during the Middle Ages. Within the building, there's a library, a large bookshop and a pleasant cafe serving mint tea. The wonderful views from the roof terrace are a good reason to prolong your visit. Open Tuesday to Sunday 10:00 to 18:00. Closed 1 May. Ⓜ Jussieu, Map 13 B2 🔟

Musée du Moyen Age

01 53 73 78 00

6 place Paul Painlevé

www.musee-moyenage.fr

The national museum of medieval art has one of the best conceivable settings for its exquisite sculptures, tapestries and enamels: a 15th century abbey building, complete with massive masonry fireplaces and Gothic doorways. Its most celebrated treasure is the cycle of six allegorical tapestries known as La Dame et la Licorne. The Hôtel de Cluny was constructed above a third century Roman thermal baths complex, elements of which are displayed within the museum. Even if you are not visiting, you can still marvel at the surviving walls outside, among the medieval-themed gardens. The museum lays on free concerts on Friday lunchtimes and Saturday afternoons. Open daily (except Tuesdays) from 09:15 to 17:45. Closed 1 January, 1 May and 25 December. Ⓜ Cluny – La Sorbonne, Map 12 E2 **20**

Musée National d'Histoire Naturelle
01 40 51 91 39
Jardin des Plantes
www.mnhn.fr

Set within the fertile grounds of the Jardin des Plantes, this isn't one museum, but three. Taken together, the Galeries de Paléontologie et d'Anatomie Comparée and the Galerie de Minéralogie et de Géologie are world class collections, but can seem a little dry compared with the Grande Galerie de l'Évolution. Here, the fine 19th century, glass-roofed building has been given the modern museum treatment. Educational, upbeat exhibitions (in tone, if not always content) range over biodiversity and man's impact on his environment. The star of the show remains the parade of African wildlife on the first floor. Open daily (except Tuesday) from 10:00 to 17:00 (until 18:00 in summer). Closed 1 May. Ⓜ Place Monge, Map 15 F2 **21**

St-Séverin
01 42 34 93 50
3 rue des Prêtres St Séverin
www.saint-severin.com

Begun in the 12th century, but owing much to the 15th, this is one of the Left Bank's oldest – and loveliest – churches. It's famous for its flamboyant Gothic vaulting which culminates in bravura carving in a final 'palm tree' column. A vibrant stained glass window by the 20th century artist Jean Bazaine is also a feature. Free choral recitals take place sporadically in summer. Open daily from 11:00 to 19:30.

Ⓜ Cluny – La Sorbonne, Map 12 E2 **22**

If you only do one thing in...
The Latin Quarter

Visit the Panthéon (p.87), its tombs and treasures and stunning vista will delight.

Best for...

Eating: Run by a dedicated husband and wife team, L'AOC (p.210) is a traditional bistro serving up some of the best rotisserie and home-made terrines in Paris. A carnivore's delight.

Drinking: Enjoy mint tea – and a stunning view – on the rooftop terrace of the sleek Institut du Monde Arabe (p.88).

Shopping: Get among the bustle at the weekly Sunday market on lively rue Mouffetard (map 15 C1).

Culture: Browse the crammed shelves at Shakespeare & Co (37 rue de la Bûcherie, 01 43 25 40 93), an institution for the expat literary set since 1951.

Families: Visit orangutans and red pandas at the Ménagerie du Jardin des Plantes (p.85), one of the oldest zoos in the world.

Louvre, Tuileries & Opéra

This area is bourgeois life at its best. Eat icecream in the Tuileries gardens, take in a night at the opera or spend days exploring centuries of art in the Louvre.

Begun by François I on the site of a medieval fortress, the Louvre grew ever more imposing until Louis XIV upped sticks for the fresh air of Versailles. Luckily, the Sun King still found time to commission the transformation of the Jardins des Tuileries, whose curvy stone nymphs and shady cafes make it a favourite spot to saunter or sit. The roar of traffic from place de la Concorde quickly dies away as you enter this chestnut-lined haven, its wide gravel paths are a magnet for visitors.

Nearby is the elaborately embellished Opéra Garnier (completed in 1875) and the *grands magasins* of Printemps (p.171) and Galeries Lafayette (p.170). A short stroll away, grandeur meets *gourmandise* at the place de la Madeleine. Dwarfed somewhat by the Église de la Madeleine, this busy square is populated by upmarket *traiteurs* such as Fauchon and Hédiard (p.173).

For **restaurants and bars** in the area, see p.216 For **shopping**, see p.168.

Jardin des Tuileries
Rue de Rivoli   www.paris.fr
This is the quintessential formal French garden. Insulated from the noise of the traffic, it's an urban haven with its

Jardin des Tuileries

avenues of pollarded chestnuts, circular ponds and statues. It takes its name from the tilemakers' quartier which stood here until it was cleared by Marie de Médicis. The park retains the essential form laid down by Le Nôtre, who landscaped it for Louis XIV. Haul up one of the sought-after metal chairs and spend an hour reading or people-watching. The children's painted sailboats are an institution and can be rented and raced around the fountain pond. The somewhat newer summer ferris wheel offers grand views over the Champs-Élysées. Don't miss the wild garden with its life-sized fallen bronze tree. Ⓜ Tuileries, Map 8 F1 🅱🅱

Jardin du Palais Royal

Place Colette   www.monument-paris.com

Opposite the north wing of the Louvre lie the hidden gardens of the Palais Royal. The regent's great-grandson, Louis Philip II, Duke of Orléans, made himself popular in Paris during the Revolution when he opened the gardens of the Palais-Royal to all Parisians, employing the neoclassical architect Victor Louis to rebuild the structures around the palace gardens and enclose it with regular colonnades. Today it remains a tranquil hideaway from the bustle outside. A few luxury boutiques back onto the garden and are definitely worth a shop. Ⓜ Palais Royale-Musée du Louvre, Map 5 C4 🅱🅱

La Madeleine   01 44 51 69 00

Place de la Madeleine   www.eglise-lamadeleine.com

Rather like the Basilique de Sainte-Geneviève (today the Panthéon), this church suffered a crisis of purpose when

Revolution struck; there were even proposals that the part-built church should be used as a marketplace. In 1806, Napoleon commissioned Barthélemy Vignon's design for a Grecian-style temple surrounded by Corinthian columns to honour the Grande Armée. As it happened, Napoleon was long dead before the project reached fruition (the church was consecrated in 1845). The interior is grand but rather gloomy under the domes and polychrome marble. The organ is exceptional; St-Saëns and Fauré were both organists here. In the cupola above the altar, Jules-Claude Ziegler's frieze puts a very First Empire slant on the history of Christianity, with Napoleon centre-stage. Open daily from 09:00 to 19:00.

Ⓜ Madeleine, Map 4 E3 **25**

Musée de l'Orangerie
Jardin des Tuileries

01 44 77 80 07
www.musee-orangerie.fr

Built as a winter hothouse for the citrus trees that surrounded the Palais des Tuileries, the Orangerie feels lighter and airier than ever, thanks to the extensive use of glass as part of the museum's modern revamp. For most visitors the real magnet is Monet's cycle of eight Nymphéas (water lilies), painted towards the end of his life at his garden in Giverny. If you can tear yourself away, you'll also find works here by Cézanne, Renoir, Modigliani, Matisse, Picasso and others. Advance booking is recommended. The museum has its own bookshop. The museum opens daily (except Tuesdays) from 12:30 to 19:00 and until 21:00 on Fridays.

Ⓜ Tuileries, Map 8 E1 **26**

Musée des Arts Décoratifs

01 44 55 57 50
www.lesartsdecoratifs.fr

107-111 rue de Rivoli

A 19th century wing of the Louvre unites an ensemble of impressive museums, the latest and most lavish of which is Musée des Arts Décoratifs. The museum charts the history of (mainly French) design from the Middle Ages to Philippe Starck. If time is limited, make a beeline for the 10 superb period rooms, but don't miss Jeanne Lanvin's art deco salon – in her trademark Lanvin-blue. Also housed here is the Musée de la Publicité, an archive of thousands of posters, TV and cinema adverts that form the basis of its temporary, themed exhibitions. Last, but by no means least, le Musée de la Mode et du Textile conserves a vast wardrobe, elements of which parade into view in the course of its temporary exhibition (check the website for updates). Within the building, the Saut du Loup restaurant is a class act, as is the design shop on the ground floor. Open Tuesday to Friday from 11:00 to 18:00 (Thursday until 21:00); Saturday to Sunday from 10:00 to 18:00. Ⓜ Palais Royal Musée du Louvre, Map 9 B1 27

Musée du Louvre

01 40 20 50 50
www.louvre.fr

Rue de Rivoli

The Louvre became a public museum under Napoleon and, with 35,000 works of art and artefacts under its roof and a programme of major temporary exhibitions, it ranks high among the world's greatest museums. Star attractions include the Venus de Milo, Michelangelo's slaves, Géricault's arresting tableau *The Raft of the Medusa* (based on a grisly true shipwreck story) and, of course, Da Vinci's Mona Lisa.

Musée du Louvre

The permanent collection enshrines everything from Egyptian antiquities to Romantic masters and more, while the grandeur of the former royal palace adds a dimension of its own. To skip the queues, buy your tickets from the machines below ground in the Carrousel du Louvre mall. The exhibits are spread across three wings (Sully, Denon, Richelieu); get your bearings with a colour-coded map available from the information desk. Entry to the permanent collection is free on the first Sunday of the month. Open: Monday, Thursday, Saturday, Sunday from 09:00 to 18:00; Wednesday and Friday from 09:00 to 22:00. Closed on Tuesdays.

Ⓜ Louvre Rivoli, Map 9 C2 🄬

Musée Grévin

10 blvd Montmartre

01 47 70 85 05
www.grevin.com

It is pricey at €18, it's kitsch, but it's also lots of fun – opened in 1882, this waxwork museum was such a sensation that it soon became Paris' most visited site after the Louvre. Times have moved on since then, but it remains a showy institution. One of the highlights isn't wax at all, but the Palais des Mirages, an ingenious lights-and-mirrors set piece fabricated for the Exposition Universelle of 1900. Aside from the icons and celebs you know well, here's where to test your knowledge of popular French culture. Do you know your Gérard Jugnot from your Gérard Dépardieu? Open Monday to Friday from 10:00 to 18:30; Saturday to Sunday 10:00 to 19:00. Ⓜ Grands Boulevards, Map 5 D2 **29**

Opéra Garnier

Place de la Opéra

08 92 89 90 90
www.opera-de-paris.fr

Charles Garnier was a virtual unknown when he landed the job of building a modern opera to embellish the new-look Second Empire city. A string of setbacks (not least the war with Prussia and the Commune) meant that it wasn't finished until 1875. In a style that defies neat definition (other than 'more is more'), it proved to be worth the wait. Inside, the Grand Foyer makes abundant use of multi-hued marble, sculptures and paintings, while the auditorium – sumptuous with its red velvet boxes – boasts a ceiling painted by Chagall in 1964. If you can't fit in a performance, a visit is the next best thing. Open daily 10:00 to 18:00 except during matinees. Closed 1 January and 1 May. Ⓜ Opéra, Map 5 A2 **30**

St-Germain l'Auxerrois

01 42 60 13 96

Rue de l'Admiral de Coligny

A church with a long history, the mainly 15th century St-Germain l'Auxerrois was built over a much earlier structure. The bell tower dates from the 12th century, though it was given the Gothic treatment in the 19th. Among the church's treasures are two exquisitely carved Flemish retables, stained glass from the 16th century, and a magnificent canopied wooden bench, designed by Le Brun for Louis XIV. Its proximity to the Louvre made this a very royal church from the 14th century. It's also infamously remembered as the church that rang its bell in August 1572 to signal the start of the St Bartholomew's Day Massacre. Open daily from 09:00 to 19:00. Ⓜ Pont Neuf, Map 9 D3 **31**

St-Roch

01 42 44 13 20

296 rue St-Honoré

Seen from the street, the baroque facade is misleading: this is a big church, almost as wide as Notre-Dame. Work began in 1653 by Jacques Lemercier (who was responsible for some galleries of the Louvre), but funds ran dry and it wasn't finished until 1740. Inside, you'll find the tombs of Diderot, Corneille and Le Nôtre, as well as some splendid works of art, not least Michel Anguier's marble *Nativity*. In 1796, the steps were the scene of a showdown between Royalists and the Conventionalists, led by an ambitious young Napoleon. Two hundred people were left dead and wounded, shot at close range. The rest, as they say, is history. Open daily from 08:00 to 19:00. Ⓜ Tuileries, Map 9 A1 **32**

If you only do one thing in...
The Louvre, Tuileries & Opéra

Walk through the Louvre's cobbled square (p.92), stop for a coffee in the Tuilerie gardens (p.216) and continue on over to the gilded Opéra (p.216).

Best for...

Eating: Book a table at Michelin star restaurant Senderens (9 place de la Madeleine, 01 42 65 22 90).

Drinking: Snare a terrace table at Le Cafè Marly (p.218) – the view is worth the price.

Culture: Visit the Grand Rex (1 Boulevard Poissonnière). Opened in 1932, it remains one of the great surviving art deco cinemas.

Shopping: Five minutes from the Louvre lie rue St-Honoré (map 9 B2) and Faubourg St-Honoré (map 4 D3), arguably the city's most glamorous streets.

Families: Give the kids a history lesson they won't forget at Paris Story (www.paris-story.com).

Clockwise from top left: St-Germain l'Auxerrois, Interior of Opéra Garnier, Musée du Louvre

Montmartre & Pigalle

Montmartre's tourist-trodden lofty heights and art-filled squares descend into Pigalle, a raunchier district home to the Moulin Rouge and lively bars.

Perched atop the Butte Montmartre, Sacré Cœur is the city's most conspicuous landmark, floating palely into view just when you least expect it. Begun as a memorial to the losses of the 1870-71 Franco-Prussian War, this Byzantine fantasy wasn't finished until after the first world war. With its artistic heritage and stunning views, the surrounding village attracts tourists by the convoy. But don't let that deter you from exploring the 'real' Montmartre, whose crumbling villas and ivy-clad cul-de-sac were the backdrop for the hit movie, Amelie. It's worth running the gauntlet of artists in place du Tertre, if only to compare it with the authenticity as you head towards Caulaincourt. To the south is Pigalle, a slightly seamy neighbourhood that is the home to The Moulin Rouge (www.moulinrouge.fr), birthplace of the can-can.

*For **restaurants and bars** in the area, see p.228. For **shopping**, see p.163.*

Cimetière de Montmartre

ave Rachel   www.pariscemeteries.com

Located west of the Butte, this cemetery was built in the hollow of an old quarry, opening for business in 1825. The cemetery epitomises the artsy, quixotic, gentle, almost whimsical Paris that every romantic visitor secretly cherishes.

A popular tourist destination, it is the final resting place for many famous artists who lived and worked in the area. Open Monday to Saturday from 08:00 to 17:30; Sunday and public holidays from 09:00 to 17:30. Hours extend by half an hour in the summer. Ⓜ Abbesses, Map 2 A1 **44**

Musée de l'Érotisme

01 42 58 28 73

72 blvd de Clichy

www.musee-erotisme.com

Where does erotica end and porn begin? This eclectic museum doesn't attempt an answer, but its seven floors display everything from ancient fertility symbols to chastity belts, from naughty nuns to Degas' Scenes from a Brothel. The upper floors are devoted to modern art; exhibitions change regularly. On the fourth floor, there are fascinating insights into life at exclusive Parisian bordellos such as le Chabanais, whose clientele included the future king of England, Edward VII. Open daily 10:00 to 02:00. Ⓜ Blanche, Map 2 B3 **45**

Musée de la Vie Romantique

01 55 31 95 67

16 rue Chaptal

www.vie-romantique.paris.fr

Ary Scheffer may have slipped into obscurity, but the green-shuttered villa the Dutch romantic artist lived in is a shrine to the arts and literature that flourished here in the 1830s. The area became known as the New Athens, partly as a result of the neoclassical architectural touches favoured hereabouts. Scheffer's bohemian guests included Liszt and Chopin and his mistress, the novelist, George Sand. The museum contains a number of her documents, mementos and watercolours, but the period rooms are the main appeal. In summer, the tearoom extends out into the pretty courtyard. The museum is free but there's a fee for the temporary exhibitions. Open Tuesday to Sunday from 10:00 to 18:00. Ⓜ Pigalle, Map 2 B4 46

Musée de Montmartre
01 46 06 61 11

12, rue Cortot   www.museedemontmartre.fr

Just along from Montmartre's tiny vineyard and the Lapin Agile, this pretty white villa with its shuttered windows was home to Renoir, Raoul Dufy, Suzanne Valadon and her son, Utrilllo. Drawings, posters and artefacts, including an original 'zinc' evoke the era of *guinguettes* and absinthe. As well as offering a tantalising glimpse into the artistic milieu that flourished here between the 1880s and the first world war, the museum contains exhibits on the redoubtable figure of the Commune, Louise Michel, and the 18th century porcelain factory at neighbouring Clignancourt. Open Tuesday to Sunday from 10:00 to 12:30 and 13:30 to 18:00.

Ⓜ Lamarck – Caulaincourt, Map 2 D1 47

Sacré-Cœur
01 53 41 89 00

Montmartre   www.sacre-coeur-montmartre.com

The city skyline wouldn't be the same without Sacré-Cœur. Originally commissioned after the bloodshed of the Franco-Prussian War and the Commune of 1871, it was consecrated in 1919. The structure was inspired by Istanbul's Hagia Sofia, and the Byzantine theme continues inside with extensive mosaics. There's a charge to climb the dome between 09:00 and 19:00 (18:00 in winter). Open daily 06:00 to 23:00, last entry at 22:15. Ⓜ Lamarck – Caulaincourt, Map 2 E1 48

Sacré-Cœur

If you only do one thing in...

Montmartre & Pigalle

Climb up to Sacré-Cœur (p.104) and admire the stunning vista of the city.

Best for...

Eating: Journey through the quartier's winding, cobblestone streets to discover Le Basilic (229), an intimate, ivy covered nook dating back to 1830. French cuisine is the speciality.

Families: Mix fun and culture on the funiculaire de Montmartre, an automatic cabin that mounts Sacré-Cœur's summit by rail.

Sightseeing: Take the opportunity to delve into the quirky backstreets of Montmartre.

Shopping: Visit rue Abbesses on Sunday mornings (map 2 B2), for the lively weekly street market.

Culture: The Musée de la Vie Romantique (p.103) is a gem, with period rooms and a lovely *salon-de-thé*.

St-Germain des Prés & Odéon

With leafy boulevards, beautiful shops and ancient churches, this is one of the city's prettiest *quartiers*. Parisians and tourists battle it out to stake their claim.

This is a lively and attractive area, with tempting boutiques along rues Dauphine and Mazarine and a cluster of cafes around the classy food market on rue de Buci. Vying for your attention on rues Jacob, Bonaparte and l'Abbaye are interior design shops, antiquarian booksellers and Ladurée's confections. A host of private galleries on the approach towards the École des Beaux-Arts makes this an art browser's paradise. The site of St-Germain's medieval fair on rue Lobineau is now an upmarket shopping arcade, while the fashion boutiques that have colonised place St-Sulpice wouldn't look amiss on avenue Montaigne. Dominating the square, the Église St-Sulpice was begun in 1646 but took over a century to complete, which may go some way to explaining its two contrasting towers. While you're down this end of town, further along the metro on line 4, Les Catacombes offer a gorier insight into the city's history.

*For **restaurants and bars** in the area, see p.234. For **shopping**,*
see p.161.

Musée National Eugène-Délacroix   01 44 42 86 50
6 rue de Furstenberg   www.musee-delacroix.fr
The romantic painter was in ailing health when, in 1857, he moved to this decidedly charming home in order to be

Les Deux Magots

nearer to the three murals he was painting at l'Église St-Sulpice. The setting is no less charming now. While Délacroix's most famous works, such as *Liberty leading the People*, have migrated to the Louvre, the paintings, drawings and memorabilia here afford a glimpse of the man throughout the stages of his life. Among the works, there's a rare self-portrait of the young artist posing as the ill-starred hero of Walter Scott's romantic novel, *The Bride of Lammermoor*. Delacroix's strangely enigmatic Magdalene in the Desert has pride of place. Open daily (except Tuesday) 09:30 to 17:00. Closed 1 January, 1 May and 25 December. Ⓜ Mabillon, Map p.12 B1 58

Musée Zadkine

01 55 42 77 20

100 bis rue d'Assas

www.paris.fr

Russian born Ossip Zadkine was one of the first sculptors to apply cubism to sculpture, and he lived and worked in this house from 1928 until his death in 1967. It's a tiny museum and the discreet entrance is easily missed. A handful of rooms testify to the apparent ease with which Zadkine moved between media, from gouache to wood and bronze. The works have a sensuous tactile appeal and there are more displayed in the garden. Entrance to the permanent collection is free. Open Tuesday to Sunday 10:00 to 18:00. Closed public holidays. Ⓜ Vavin, Map 14 E2 59

St-Germain des Prés

01 55 42 81 33

3 place St-Germain-des-Prés

www.eglise-sgp.org

This is the oldest church in Paris. Only a few stones remain from the original Benedictine abbey and basilica built here in around 550AD, and in which the Merovingian kings were buried. The rest, including the tower, dates back to the 11th and 12th centuries. Look out for the tomb of René Descartes – and the early masons' marks near the entrance. Open Monday to Saturday 08:00 to 19:45; Sunday 09:00 to 20:00.

Ⓜ St-Germain-des-Prés, Map 12 B2 **60**

St-Sulpice

Place St-Sulpice

01 46 33 21 78

www.paroisse-saint-sulpice-paris.org

When it emerges from its restorers' scaffolding, St-Sulpice boasts a fine Italianate portico and two slightly mismatched, though splendid, towers (its construction took more than a century from 1646). Just inside are three frescos painted by Delacroix – in a corner of *Jacob Wrestling with the Angel* is what looks like the artist's straw hat. Notice also the shell-shaped fonts sculpted by Pigalle, and an 18th century obelisk, part of a gnomon, or astronomy measuring device. Open daily 07:30 to 19:30. Ⓜ St-Sulpice, Map 12 B2 **61**

Les Catacombes de Paris

1 ave Colonel Henri-Rol-Tanguy

01 43 22 47 63

www.musees.paris.fr

It's estimated that the remains of six million people lie here, including those of Robespierre and his henchmen. As you enter, there's a long, winding descent to the tunnels, where skulls, femurs and the rest are tightly and anonymously packed in walls. It's a chilly walk of a few kilometres, with macabre memento moris along the way. Entry is €7. Open Tuesday to Sunday from 09:30 to 16:00.

Ⓜ Denfert Rochereau, Map 1 C4

If you only do one thing in...

St-Germain des Prés & Odéon

Walk along boulevard St-Germain and take in the oldest church in Paris: St-Germain des Prés (p.110).

Best for...

Eating: Join the queue outside master pâtissier Pierre Hermé's at 72 rue Bonaparte in order to snare your taste of dessert heaven.

Drinking: Sip coffee among the ghosts of Sartre, Beauvoir, Camus and Hemingway at Café de Flore (p.233) and Les Deux Magots (p.236).

Sightseeing: Stroll towards the Right Bank along the romantic pont des Arts as the sun sets and take in the breathtaking views.

Relaxation: Lose yourself among the well-dressed boutiques of rue Jacob and rue des Saints-Pères.

Outdoor: Make your way to Jardin du Luxembourg (p.86), a haven of greenery and leisure pursuits.

Trocadéro & Les Invalides

These *quartiers* combine military history and tourist chic. Bask in the splendour of the Iron Lady or picnic on manicured lawns around Les Invalides.

Crowning Trocadéro Hill is the creamy-white, art deco Palais de Chaillot, built for the Exposition Universelle of 1937. By day, the broad terrace between the two pavilions throngs with tourists and souvenir hawkers. By night, flanked by the gargantuan statues of Apollo and Hercules, there's no finer spot to admire a shimmering Eiffel Tower. You may tire of its image on everything from publicity campaigns to tea towels, but up close the monument never fails to impress.

Beyond, the regimented flowerbeds of the Champ de Mars were once the parade ground for the École Militaire, built under Louis XV to train soldiers (including, eventually, a young Napoleon). The golden-domed Hôtel des Invalides was built as a home for Louis XIV's wounded soldiers, though its main claim to fame is now as the resting place of Napoleon's tomb. The green space out front is a nice spot to take a break from the frenetic pace of museum visiting.

Eiffel Tower

01 44 11 23 23
www.tour-eiffel.fr

Quai Branly

Brilliant, graceful, emblematic – even so, the Eiffel Tower provoked a furore when it went up in 1889 (for the Exposition Universelle) on the centenary of the Revolution. Many felt it jarred badly with the existing monuments of the day. Pre-fabricated at Gustave Eiffel's foundry at Levallois-Perret, the tower took only 21 months to assemble, a remarkable achievement for the time. At 276 metres, it was the world's tallest building, and remained so for decades. However, the tower wasn't meant to stay up indefinitely. By the mid 1920s, it was in such disrepair that a trickster, Victor Lustig, managed to 'sell' it to a scrap dealer. It now welcomes around six million visitors each year. To join them, try coming late in the day when you're more likely to avoid the queues. Tickets are sold at the base; ascent is by hydraulic lift (or stairs to the second floor). From here, the 360° view extends up to 50 miles when visibility is good. Prolong your visit with a splurge at the Restaurant Jules Verne (p.246). The top floor contains Eiffel's cosy office. The first floor becomes a garden terrace in summer, and an ice rink in winter. Opening times: 1 January to 14 June and 2 September to 31 June, 09:30 to 23:00; 15 June to 1 September, 09:00 to midnight. Ⓜ Bir-Hakeim, Map 7 C3 49

Les Égouts de Paris
Pont d'Alma

01 53 68 27 81
www.paris.fr

A fascinating and only slightly whiffy museum, this is just a taster, so to speak, of the city's 2,100km of underground sewers. The network replicates the city, its channels bearing the names of the streets above. As well as an insight into the heavy duty dredging technology deployed to keep thing moving along, there's a display on the history of the sewers, begun under Napoleon but uncharted during the Haussmann era. This dangerous task was the inspiration for Victor Hugo's descriptions of Valjean's subterranean adventure in *Les Misérables*. Open daily (except Thursday and Friday): May to September, from 11:00 to 17:00; October to April, from 11:00 to 16:00. Closed for two weeks mid-January.

Ⓜ Pont de l'Alma, Map 7 E1 **50**

Les Invalides
Quai d'Orsay

01 44 42 40 69
www.invalides.org

Founded as a war veteran's home by Louis XIV in 1670, les Invalides was built by Jules Hardouin-Mansart, of Versailles fame. It's a large complex, comprising two churches, the Musée de l'Armée, the Musée de l'Ordre de la Libération and the Musée des Plans-Reliefs (a collection of scale models of cities begun by Vauban, Louis XIV's military architect). A part of the complex remains a hospital to this day. The gilt Église du Dôme was built for the king's exclusive use. Since 1840, it's been a shrine to Napoleon, whose red porphyry tomb lies surrounded by monumental evocations of greatness and grief. Open daily: April to September, from 10:00 to 18:00; October to March, from 10:00 to 17:00. Closed the first Monday of the month. Ⓜ Invalides, Map 8 B4 **51**

Musée Baccarat
Place des Etats-Unis

01 40 22 11 00
www.baccarat.fr

Part of the former *hôtel particulier* of the Vicomtesse de Noailles has been transformed into a showcase for the house of Baccarat, a company that has been producing some of the world's finest crystal since 1764. It's more gallery than museum, but you don't have to be a connoisseur to be blown

Napoleon's tomb, Les Invalides

away by the masterpieces created for royalty, or the 19th century Expositions Universelles, designed by the likes of Georges Chevalier. The elegant interior comes courtesy of Philippe Starck. Naturally, there's a gift shop and a fabulous restaurant called Cristal Room. Open Monday, Wednesday, Saturday from 10:00 to 18:00. Ⓜ Boissière, Map 3 C3 **52**

Musée d'Orsay

1 rue de Bellechasse

01 40 49 48 14
www.musee-orsay.fr

This museum concentrates exclusively on art produced between 1848 and 1914. The elegant building is a converted Belle Époque train station flooded with natural light. A sculpture gallery occupies the central aisle where the railway tracks once ran. The galleries unfold more or less chronologically through the Romantics, Symbolists and the Barbizon landscape group, embracing early photography and decorative arts along the way. The upper floor is devoted to Impressionist and Post-Impressionist masterpieces, among them Van Gogh's *Chambre à Arles* and Manet's *Déjeuner sur l'Herbe*. The restaurant dazzles under great crystal chandeliers; there's also a cafe and a bookshop. Entry is free on the first Sunday of the month. Open Tuesday to Sunday from 09:30 to 18:00. Ⓜ Musée d'Orsay, Map 8 F2 **53**

Musée de l'Art Moderne de la Ville de Paris

11 ave du Président Wilson

01 53 67 40 00
www.paris.fr

Like the Palais de Chaillot, the grandiose Palais de Tokyo was built for the 1937 Exposition Universelle. In 2006, it opened its doors to reveal the city's own modern art collection with an impressive show of Fauvists, Cubists and a varied programme of temporary shows. Near the entrance, Raoul Dufy's vibrant set piece, *La Fée Electricité*, fills an entire room. In the Palais' adjacent wing is the new Site de Création – open-plan, minimally finished and with acres of space for edgy installations and performances. There's a funky cafe and a bookshop, piled high with the latest must-have arty volumes. Open Tuesday to Sunday from 10:00 to 18:00 (Wednesday until 22:00). Ⓜ Iéna, Map 7 D1 **54**

Musée du Quai-Branly

01 56 61 70 00
37 Quai Branly   www.quaibranly.fr

Opened with a big splash in 2006, this showcase of non-European art and artefacts unites some of the choicest collections of the Musées des Arts d'Afrique et d'Océanie and the Musée de l'Homme (the latter currently exhibits temporarily while it awaits a further metamorphosis). This riverside complex is a show-stopping combination of glass and greenery (some 18,000 square metres of it), designed by renowned architect Jean Nouvel. Once inside, winding footbridges connect the four continents of Oceania, Asia, Africa and America, inviting you to set out on your own journey of exploration. Very much ex-President Chirac's baby, the museum has a huge visual impact, right down to details such as the modern aboriginal paintings that adorn the bookshop. There's a garden cafe and a posh terrace restaurant with panoramic views. Open Tuesday to Sunday from 10:00 to 18:30 (Thursday until 21:30). Ⓜ Pont de l'Alma , Map 7 D2 **55**

Musée Galliera

01 56 52 86 03
www.galliera-paris.fr

10 ave Pierre 1er de Serbie

A trio of larger-than-life photos graces the wall of this somewhat overblown 19th century palace, named after the Duchess who lived here. In case you're in any doubt, the Galliera is dedicated to fashion. Its huge collection of almost 100,000 garments and accessories spans three centuries and represents the great names in French couture up to the present day. The museum is only open during exhibitions or when a thematic selection is on show. Such events are invariably stylish and normally stay for around four months. Check the museum's website for information.

Ⓜ léna, Map 3 D4 **56**

Musée Guimet

01 56 52 53 00
www.museeguimet.fr

6 place d'léna

Like the Musée Cernuschi, this collection of oriental artefacts owes its existence to one man, Émile Guimet, a 19th century industrialist who travelled extensively in Asia. His collection forms a fraction of what is now on show, ranging from exquisite silk kimonos to Javan deities. Inside the building, Guimet's exotic structure opens up like a Chinese box, thanks to a spacious, modern transformation that makes much play of natural light. The museum has its own restaurant and library. The Buddhist Pantheon is not to be missed, complete with Japanese garden and tearoom, nearby at number 19 (entry is free). The museum itself is free on the first Sunday of the month. Open daily (except Tuesday) 10:00 to 18:00.

Ⓜ léna, Map 3 C4 **57**

Eiffel Tower

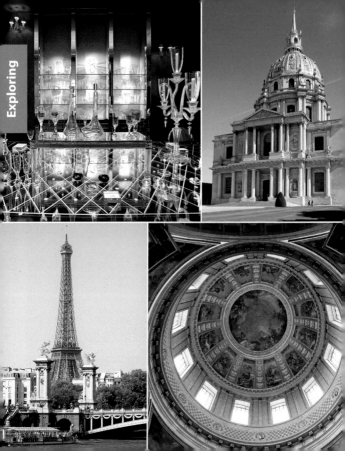

If you only do one thing in...
Trocadéro & Les Invalides

Stroll through the colonnades at Les Invalides and visit Napoleon's tomb (p.114).

Best for...

Eating: Marie Ann Cantin's fromagerie (p.173) on the rue Cler is a must-do for cheese fans.

Drinking: Enjoy the view of the Eiffel Tower from the terrace of Café de l'Homme (17 place du Trocadéro).

Families: The Cinéaqua has an aquarium, cinema and educational shows to keep children entertained (www.cineaqua.com).

Culture: The Musée du Quai Branly (p.119) showcases collections from Africa, Asia and the Americas.

Outdoor: Adjacent to les Invalides, the gardens at the Musée Rodin are a delight on a mild day (www.musee-rodin.fr).

Clockwise from top left: Musée Baccarat, Les Invalides, Dome at Les Invalides, Eiffel Tower

Further Out

Drag yourself from the charming inner-city Parisian streets to these worthwhile addresses, just a short trip by train from the centre.

Greater Paris

There are more than one or two worthwhile attractions away from the main tourist thoroughfares. In the 19th arrondissement visit the Parc de la Villette (metro Porte de la Villette). The funky, thematic gardens might baffle grown-ups, but they're a hit with kids – all the more for features such as the 80 metre long dragon slide. At its northern edge, you'll find La Cité des Sciences et de l'Industrie, a vast, intelligently run museum with lots of hands-on appeal. Outside, two cinemas and a 1957 submarine vie for your attention. Across the park, the Musée de la Musique is also one of a kind. Along with a concert hall and library, the polished concrete building houses a major collection of instruments, most of which you can hear courtesy of the free audio guides.

Rising to the east of the Canal St-Martin, multi-ethnic Belleville and its more upmarket neighbour, Ménilmontant, ooze character (metros Belleville and Ménilmontant). Settled by successive waves of immigrants, Belleville is the Paris that Haussmann left alone. Lower Belleville is a tumult of humanity shopping for halal meat and oriental silk slippers. Uphill, the real village around St-Jean-Baptiste-de-Belleville has a quaintly provincial feel, in sharp contrast to the concrete uglies of nearby place des Fêtes. The views from Belleville's modest, vine-covered park give Montmartre a run for its money, but by far the most appealing green space here is the Parc des Buttes-Chaumont (metro Buttes Chaumont). Built on the site of a former quarry, this is perhaps Haussmann's sole legacy to Belleville. Its rambling paths, lake and fanciful belvedere give it real charm, without the crowds you'll find elsewhere. Also in this corner of Paris is the cimetière du Père Lachaise (metro Père Lachaise), where fans can visit the graves of Jim Morrison and Oscar Wilde.

Over in the 14th, Montparnasse (metro Montparnasse Bienvenue) still trades somewhat on its artistic heyday, though the modern concrete buildings along avenue du Maine might make you wonder why. The 210m Tour Montparnasse doesn't help matters either; from the outside it's pretty dull but the view from the 56th floor is one of the best in the city. Nearby and occupying the southern corner of place Denfert-Rochereau is the entrance to Les Catacombes (p.111), one of the city's more macabre landmarks. A visit through its tunnels of stacked skulls is not for the squeamish, but with all those memento moris, you won't forget it in a hurry. Next door in the 15th is the large Parc André-Citroën, built on the site of the former car factory. With its colour-blocked flowers, yawning terraces and squirting jet fountains, it puts a decidedly contemporary twist on the French tradition of formal gardens. You can take a short helium balloon ride above the lawns for a view of the scaled-down Statue of Liberty (an early prototype of the New York version).

North Of Paris

Just outside the bounds of Paris at Porte de Clignancourt is the Marché St-Ouen, the city's largest flea market showcasing fashion, antiques and bric-a-brac. Take metro line 4 all the way to Porte de Clignancourt; the markets are a short stroll.

Further afield, Auvers-sur-Oise is a must for Impressionist fans. Van Gogh spent his last months here, leaving a legacy of 70 local paintings. The inn where he stayed has been restored and the *château* has a good multimedia show. By train, Auvers is an hour's ride from the Gare du Nord, with a direct service in summer. Top-notch equestrian entertainment – and a princely *château* – make an equally worthwhile outing to Chantilly (www.chantilly-tourisme.com). Last but not least, Parc Astérix offers a splashing good time. Take RER B to Charles de Gaulle airport and then a shuttle bus (www.parcasterix.fr). The park is closed from November to March. Opening hours are: April to June from 10:00 to 18:00 daily, July and August from 09:30 to 19:00 daily. In September and October the park opens from 10:00 to 18:00 Wednesdays, Saturdays and Sundays. Tickets can be purchased at RER and train stations.

East Of Paris

Disneyland Resort Paris (0825 305 300, www.disneylandparis.com) is incontestably the main draw of this area. It's just 40 minutes on RER A from the centre of Paris. It consists of Disney Village with its hotels and restaurants, Disneyland Park which is the theme parks and Walt Disney Studios, which brings the world of film and animation to life. Queues can be long so an early start is best. Hours vary but the resort is open seven days a week, Monday to Friday from 08:15 to 20:45, Saturdays from 09:00 to 19:00 and Sundays from 10:00 to 20:00 All-inclusive tickets are available at RER and metro stations.

For a fairytale setting of a different sort, the town of Provins (www.provins.net) has Unesco status for its well-preserved ramparts and underground passages. In summer, it goes to town on medieval pageantry. Count on it taking 90 minutes by train from the Gare de l'Est; less by car on the A4.

South Of Paris

On Paris' doorstep is the stupendous, 14th century Château de Vincennes (metro line 1). Further out, Fontainebleau (www.fontainebleau-tourisme.com) is a 40 minute drive or an hour by train from Gare de Lyon. The *château* alone is a daytrip, but there's a full weekend's worth here if combined with forest rambles or a visit to the town of Barbizon. When there, make the daytrip to Vaux-le-Vicomte (www.vaux-le-vicomte.com), a *château* so ravishing it inspired the envy of Louis XIV.

West Of Paris

Topping the visiting list is Versailles (www.versailles-tourime.com); the gardens alone are worth a visit on a sunny day. At the other end of the architectural spectrum, the business district of La Défense centred on la Grande Arche (metro line 1 or RER A) makes a surprisingly good stroll with its sculptures and quirky landscaping. Finally, the upmarket suburb of St-Germain-en-Laye is entrenched in history, and a mere 20 minutes away (RER A). The former royal *château* houses the national archaeology collection (01 39 10 13 00).

Tours & Sightseeing

There's more than one way to view Paris, as the city's enormous number of organised tours attest; stroll, pedal, sail or fly, the choice is yours.

Bicycle Tours

Fat Tire Bike Tours

24 rue Edgar Fauré

01 56 58 10 54
www.fattirebiketoursparis.com

The sister company of City Segway Tours and Classic Walks, Fat Tire runs four-hour bike tours encompassing all the main sights and providing upbeat and interesting insights along the way. No reservations are needed and tours still run if it's raining. Departure is from the southern pillar of the Eiffel Tower. Evening tours are a fun alternative; they're slightly more expensive and last up to an hour longer.

Ⓜ Bir-Hakeim, Map 1 B3

Paris Charms & Secrets

place Vendôme

01 40 29 00 00
www.parischarmssecrets.com

This is a bike tour – but not as you know it. These nippy, battery-powered bikes take the toil out of hills, enabling groups to cover over 20 kilometres with minimum effort, and take in a number of the city's lesser-known sites. Bikes are easy to use and the guides are well-versed. Groups of up to 20 bikes set out from the place Vendôme three times daily. Daytime tours start at 09:30 and 14:30, and last around four hours while evening tours depart at 20:00 and last three hours. Ⓜ Opéra, Map 5 B2

Boat & Yacht Tours

Bateaux-Mouches
01 42 25 96 10

Port de la Conférence,
Port de l'Alma
www.bateaux-mouches.fr

The formulaic sightseeing cruise accompanied by a whistle-stop commentary in eight languages may not stoke your engine, but the veteran Seine-cruise company also offers dinner, lunch and – for a price – romantic cruises. Times and costs vary according to tours; see the website for details.
Ⓜ Alma Marceau, Map 7 E1

Batobus
08 25 05 01 01

Porte de la Bourdonnais
www.batobus.com

This riverboat makes eight stops at strategic locations along the Seine. Operating hours vary according to the season, with the first boats setting sail at 10:00 or 10:30, and running up to 21:30 in the summer. Boats depart every 15 to 30 minutes. Tickets are available at every stop. A popular tourist option is the Paris à la carte ticket which can be used in conjunction with L'Open Tour buses. Ⓜ Bir-Hakeim, Hotel de Ville or St Michel, Map 7 D3

Canauxrama
01 42 39 15 00

Bassin de la Villette, 13 quai de la Loire www.canauxrama.com

Canauxrama offer cruises with commentary along the city's other waterway, the Canal St-Martin, built under Napoleon to facilitate access to the Seine from the eastern side of Paris. Lasting around two-and-a-half hours, cruises pass through some of the city's up-and-coming areas, under bridges and through four double locks. You'll also glide through stretches of tunnel, brightened by Keïchi Tahara's luminous installation. Timings and costs vary. **Ⓜ** Jaurès Map 1 E1

Chris River Yacht Charter   06 66 52 18 66
Various Locations   www.parisexclusiveyacht.com

Exclusive Seine river cruises are the deal here. Hop aboard a fully crewed, 30ft luxury motor yacht and enjoy gourmet snacks and champagne along the way. Cruises take two to five passengers and cost between €179 and €395 per person. Itineraries and boarding piers vary. Book two days in advance. Cruises operate May to October.

Paris Canal   01 42 40 96 97
Bassin de la Villette, 19-21 quai de la Loire
www.pariscanal.com

Paris Canal offers sightseeing cruises along the Canal St-Martin taking in a stretch of Seine and the Canal de l'Ourcq. It's a leisurely affair, with boats departing from the Quai Anatole France below the Musée d'Orsay and arriving in the Parc de la Villette two-and-a-half hours later. The commentary is in both French and English. Advance booking is recommended. Cruises operate daily from 09:30 from the Musée d'Orsay; 14:30 from Parc de la Villette. There are additional sailings during high season.

Ⓜ Assemblee National, Map 1 E1

Vedettes de Paris
Port de Suffren

01 47 05 71 29
www.vedettesdeparis.com

There's canned commentary on the one-hour sightseeing cruise, which leaves every hour from below the Eiffel Tower. The company also offers lunch, dinner and children's cruises for 'little sailors' (French commentary). Operating daily every hour: Easter to Oct, 10:00 to 22:00; November to February, 11:00 to 18:00. Ⓜ Bir-Hakeim Map 7 B4

Vedettes de Pont-Neuf
square du Vert Galant

01 46 33 98 38
www.vedettesdupontneuf.com

One of the cheapest Seine cruises, these boats ply a pleasant one-hour circuit. Discounted fares are available online. Departures are every 30 to 45 minutes in high season, every 45 minutes in winter. Don't disembark without picking up your Official VPN medal. Daily cruises: March to October, 10:00 to 22:30; November to February, 10:30 to 22:00.
Ⓜ Pont Neuf, Map 9 D4

Bus Tours

Cityrama
Various Locations

01 44 55 60 00
www.pariscityrama.com

A number of daily sightseeing tours are on offer in air-conditioned double-decker buses, with multilingual commentary. All the major tourist attractions are covered. Tours last from one-and-a-half to four-and-a-half hours, starting from €18. Reservations only.
Ⓜ Bir-Hakeim, Charles de Gaulle Etoile, Concorde, Trocadéro

Tours & Sightseeing

L'Open Tour
01 42 66 56 56
Various Locations   www.paris-opentour.com

These hop-on, hop-off open buses have the city covered pretty well with their four circuits. There's a multilingual commentary along the way. Combined passes with Batobus are available. Ⓜ Bir-Hakeim, Concorde, Hauvre-Caumartin, St Michel

Les Cars Rouges
01 5 39 59 53
Various Locations   www.carsrouges.com

These big, red, hop-on, hop-off buses offer two-and-a-quarter hour tours covering the main monuments. Commentary is multilingual and tickets are valid over two days. Starting at 09:30, departures are every eight to 15 minutes in summer; 10 to 20 minutes in winter. Last departure is at 18:00 from Trocadéro. Ⓜ Charles de Gaulle Etoile, St Michel, Trocadéro

Paris Euroscope
01 56 03 56 81
27 rue Taitbout   www.euroscope.fr

This company's out-of-town offerings range from a half-day visit to Chartres to four-day combined trips around the Normandy beaches, Mont-St-Michel and the Châteaux of the Loire, with stays in two or three-star hotels. Tours are by air-conditioned minibus, with a driver-guide. English, German, Spanish, Italian and Portuguese are offered. Map 5 C2

Paris Vision
01 42 60 30 01
214 rue de Rivoli   www.parisvision.com

Large air-conditioned bus and minibus tours are available, as well as soirées around town. The company also offers a range of day-long outings to the Loire valley and other destinations. Paris Vision organises walking tours, too. Ⓜ Tuileries, Map 9 A1

Helicopter & Plane Charters

Hélifrance
Le Bourget Airport

01 45 54 95 11
www.helifrance.fr

The 25 minute, €135 Sunday flight from Le Bourget Airport gives you an exhilarating bird's eye view of Paris, its geometry and its landmarks. Combine it with a flight over Versailles or an hour's visit to the Musée de l'Air et l'Éspace at Le Bourget (This last package departs from the Paris Héliport at Issy-les-Moulineaux). Reservation only.

Heritage Tours

Centre des Monuments Nationaux
Blvd Morland

01 44 54 19 30
www.monuments-nationaux.fr

If your French is up to it, the Visites Conférences offer incredibly informative tours. Visits range from highly focused tours of a single monument, to all-day coach excursions out of the city. Most tours cost €8 and don't require advance booking. Ⓜ Sully Morland, Map 13 E4

Paris Muse
Various Locations

06 73 77 33 52
www.parismuse.com

An educational service tailored to English-speakers, Paris Muse provides in-depth art tours for groups of four or less within some of Paris' most notable museums. The company also caters for children and family visits. Led by academically trained art historians, most tours last from 90 minutes to two hours, and start from around €70. Tours are by reservation only.

Private Tours

Paris International VIP Services   01 43 31 81 69
65 rue Pascal   www.paris-tours-guides.com

This group specialises in delivering private tours (it's credited with the Paris Office of Tourism). The company will deliver a bespoke itinerary, a guide or interpreter, a chauffeured car and will make any other bookings or arrangements necessary for a successful visit. Ⓜ Les Gobelins, Map 15 C4

Shopping Tours

Chic Shopping Paris   06 14 56 23 11
Various Locations   www.chicshoppingparis.com

CSP's tours are led by bilingual Parisians with insider knowledge of the hotspots. A wide variety of shopping themes are available, from babywear to outlet fashion or gourmet produce. Prices start at €100 per person for a tour of around four hours, excluding refreshments. Groups are limited to five people or less.

Shopping Plus   01 47 53 91 17
Various Locations   www.paris-gourmet.com

This company has been offering tours since 1990. There are three options: fashion (focusing on the Golden Triangle),

Antiques (a foray into the Carée Rive Gauche) and Interior Design (in and among the *bonnes addresses* of the Left Bank). Tours are limited to 10 people. A day tour costs €230; lunch and a coffee break are included.

Walking Tours

Ça-Se-Visite!

01 48 06 27 41

1 rue Robert Houdin

www.ca-se-visite.fr

The multi-ethnic, working class *quartiers* of eastern Paris were, until recently, well off the visitor trail. Locally run Ça-Se-Visite! has done much to change that, offering lively urban walks around the area's hidden courtyards, artists' studios and historic streets. The Saturday 'Belleville Past and Present' walk is offered in English to groups of eight people, by prior arrangement only. Ⓜ Belleville, Map 1 E2

Classic Walks

01 56 58 10 54

24 rue Edgar Fauré

www.classicwalksparis.com

The company's classic tour is a hefty hike of three-and-a-half hours, but the time flies by in the company of a locally based expatriate with lots of facts and anecdotes to share. Covering virtually all of Paris' major landmarks, this is an excellent orientation to the city as a whole. Classic Walks also runs more focused walks, for example, on Montmartre, the French Revolution and the second world war. In most cases, reservations are optional rather than necessary. Most tours start out from the company's offices in the 15th. Check the website for details. Ⓜ Dupleix, Map 7 B3

Paris Walks

Various Locations

01 48 09 21 40

www.paris-walks.com

The 'original' Paris Walks offers a diverse programme of tours led by local expats. Guides are chatty and informed, and the quartier-centred tours are a great way to deepen your acquaintance with a particular neighbourhood. Themed tours change regularly. Recent offerings have included gourmet chocolate tasting, Edith Piaf and literary Paris tours. Tours run daily between March and October, booking is unnecessary. Check the website for details.

Other Tours

4 Roues Sous 1 Parapluie

12 rue Chabanais

06 67 32 26 67

www.4-roues-sous-1parapluie.com

This young company offers tours from the comfort of the quintessential French vehicle, the Citroên 2CV. Outings range from a 90 minute sweep-around-the-sights to a tailor-made excursion lasting several hours. You name the pick-up spot. Chauffeur-driven, the cars can take a maximum of three passengers. Ⓜ Pyramides, Map 5 B4

Art Bus

52 rue Sedaine

01 47 00 90 85

www.art-process.com

The Art Process agency runs this once-monthly minibus tour of all that's new and happening in Paris' contemporary art scene. Typically, a circuit may take in commercial collections, artists' studios, art centres and alternative art spaces, and there are frequent opportunities to meet the people behind the canvases. It's a bilingual affair, takes four to five hours and costs €35. Tours depart at 11:00 on the third Saturday in the month. Places are limited and bookings are required. If you can't make the fixed dates for the minibus tour, they also offer an art limo service. Ⓜ Bastille, Chemin Vert, Voltaire

City Segway Tours

01 56 58 10 54

24 rue Edgar Fauré   www.citysegwaytours.com

American-run, this arm of Fat Tire Bike Tours is based on the curious-looking, self-balancing 'Human Transporter' – otherwise known as the Segway. Standing upright on your wheels, you glide effortlessly around in a small, guided convoy. Segways are user-friendly and require no special skill. A range of city and out-of-town tours are available, including a Paris by night tour. Generally, they last four to five hours. Tours operate from 15 February to 30 November, departing at 09:30, 14:00 and 18:30. Ⓜ Dupleix, Map 1 B3

Edible Paris

Various Locations   www.edible-paris.com

Paris-based food writer and restaurant critic Rosa Jackson provides customised, self-guided itineraries for those interested in learning where to eat out in the city. Prices start at €200 for a one day itinerary, which includes a personalised selection of shopping addresses, cafes, brasseries and restaurants, which she will reserve in advance. Ms Jackson also offers guided, tailor-made, behind-the-scenes tours for up to six people. These tours last three hours and cost €250.

Sports & Spas

Paris Action

Burn off any gastronomic excesses over a game of golf or take in the sights by rollerblade. Then, relax and indulge once more in fine French food and wine.

Parisians once eschewed gyms in favour of outdoor sports like skiing, tennis, and football (soccer). Today, however, the city has accepted a more structured and sporty lifestyle, sparking the introduction of a hoard of excellent new gyms. Pilates classes, martial arts studios and more have begun to crop up alongside the swimming pools which grace every *arrondissement*. And that's not forgetting the swathe of international sports embraced by the French: think horseball from Argentina, *'le foot'* (football) and cricket from the UK, Péteca from Brazil, and volleyball from America, just to name a few. Golf has also made its presence known, with the best courses positioned within sprinting distance of the *périphérique*.

With all the indoor, outdoor, extreme and seasonal sports that thrive in Paris, the inhabitants haven't forgotten to go Zen. Parks are as prevalent as the museums, those hankering for a massage won't be short of choices, and there are always hammams for anyone who has spent the day elbowing their way through the Louvre to get close to Mona. Nor is the past overlooked; locals partaking in *montgolfier* (ballooning), *pétanque*, and *jeu de paume* can still be found tucked into corners of the city.

Le Jardin du Luxembourg

Cooking Classes

Elegance Cooking
01 42 04 74 00

www.elegantcooking.com

Begin with a tour of the city's markets to pick up the day's freshest produce before retiring to instructor Marguerite's Paris abode for a morning of cooking and lunching in her charming courtyard. Classes are taught in English and specialise in classic French cuisine.

Promenades Gourmandes
01 42 04 74 00

www.promenadesgourmandes.com

Leading groups of six or less through gastronomic food tours and cooking classes in her Parisian apartment, Paule Caillat offers half, full and multi-day sessions specialising in French cooking. Prices vary depending on group size: half-day classes start from €230; full day classes start from €330; walking tours (no cooking) are €110; multi-day classes start at €450.

Golf

Les Bordes
02 54 87 72 13

Les Bordes, Saint Laurent-Nouan
www.lesbordes.com

Designed by Robert von Hagge, the 18 hole course was formerly a hunting estate of Baron Marcel Bich, the inventor of the Bic pen. The challenging 7,062 yard, par 72 woodland course is considered one of the finest in France and has won *Golfjournal's* Travel Oscar for Best European Golf Course. Check out the Rodin replica statues lining the driveway.

Paris Golf & Country Club
01 47 77 64 00

121 rue du Lieutenant-Colonel de Montbrison,
Rueil-Malmaison   www.pariscountryclub.com

This nine-hole, par 35 course is set within the Hippodrome
de Saint-Cloud racecourse, 2 kilometres to the west of the
Bois de Boulogne. In addition to the course, with its share of
bunkers and water hazards, there's a large 200 berth driving
range, separate pitch and putt areas, two putting greens and
zones to practise chipping and bunker play. The golf course is
open from 08:00 to 21:00 in the summer, and 08:30 to 18:30
in winter. The club also offers other sports including tennis,
volleyball, basketball, football and swimming.

Paris International Golf Club
01 30 43 36 00

2 ave du Golf, Guyancourt   www.golf-national.com

Surrounding the historic Chateau of Versailles is the famous
Albatros course at Le Golf National designed by Hubert
Chesneau and Robert Von Hagge. As a cross between a target
course and a links course, this is a clay based, lengthy (over
7,000 yards) par 72. It is not only recognised as one of the
top courses in Europe, but has also hosted the French Open.
There are three courses, but most people make a beeline for
the challenging championship Albatros.

Vaucouleurs
01 34 87 62 29

Rue de l'église, Civry la Forêt   www.vaucouleurs.fr

Located around 45km to the west of Paris, Vaucouleurs offers
two very different courses to golf enthusiasts; Les Vallons is
a real links course, 5,638 metres long with a par of 70, while

La Rivière, par 73 and 6,138 metres, is typical for this part of France. With a bar, restaurant and pro shop on-site, this is the perfect countryside course and will suit golfers of all abilities to a tee.

Rollerblading & Rollerskating

Pari-Roller

Place Raoul Dautry, Montparnasse   www.pari-roller.com

This is unadulterated street skating at its free-for-all best. Join over 10,000 people every Friday night as they blast off on a 20 mile tour from Montparnasse around the uneven paved streets of the city. Full protection is a must; these are serious skaters. For those just learning the heel-stop-and-stagger stance techniques, Sunday afternoons at Place de la Bastille won't be quite so daunting. You'll get to roll slowly with bikers, skateboarders, runners and see Paris in full daylight.

Ⓜ Montparnasse Bienvenüe, Map 14 A2 🛈

Swimming

Aquaboulevard   01 40 60 10 00

4 rue Louis Armand, Porte de Sèvres   www.aquaboulevard.com

The mammoth Aquaboulevard takes up almost 23,000 square feet, making it the biggest water park in Europe. There are 11 water slides, including the 80m Aquaplouf, an 84°F pool with rolling waves, water cannons, sauna, jacuzzis, restaurants, a hammam and cinemas. Forest Hills, Europe's largest fitness club, is also onsite providing facilities for

Rollerblading at Trocadéro

tennis, squash, racquetball, badminton and ping-pong as well as a gymnasium and faux beach. Ⓜ Balard, Map 1 A4

Piscine Joséphine-Baker   01 52 61 46 50
Bibliothèque François Mitterrand, Bercy
Josephine Baker, the actress and civil rights leader, always did make a splash so it's appropriate the city's newest pool built in the 13th *arrondissement* carries her name. Surrounded by the Seine; the pool is a floating barge of aqua with a retractable roof exposing swimmer's to the sky. Ⓜ Quai de la Gare, Map 1 E4

Ritz Health Club   01 43 16 30 60
Hotel Ritz Paris, Place Vendôme   www.ritzparis.com
Certainly the most beautiful place to do backstroke, the *piscine* at this luxe hotel's health club, with its marble

Corinthian columns and whirlpool, feels like something out of ancient Rome. The pool has jet-streams as well as underwater sound for complete relaxation. Afterwards, walk up the stairs under the fluted columns to the Mezzanine bar, order a fruit cocktail (the orange and carrot juice is a bit of heaven) and enjoy a light lunch. Ⓜ Opéra, Map 4 F4 ☑

Tennis

Municipal Courts   01 43 25 79 18
Jardin du Luxembourg, Montparnasse
Paris has 41 municipal tennis centres, with a variety of outdoor and covered courts and assorted playing surfaces on offer. The most popular are at the Jardin du Luxembourg (six in all) and Bois de Vincennes in the south-east of the city. To play you'll need to reserve a court online in advance. Otherwise, you can take your chances and turn up and wait for a court to become free. Visit www.tennisparis.fr for more information and to book a court.

Ⓜ Luxembourg, Map 14 F1 ☑

Wine Tasting

La Dernière Goutte   01 43 29 11 62
6 rue de Bourbon le Chateau, Odéon www.lademieregoutte.com
Stop in this shop to buy booze, join free wine tastings on Saturdays or even to meet a featured wine grower who will educate you in the joys of the grape. The store is small but the atmosphere is lovely. American-born Juan Sanchez knows

Ô Château

how to pick excellent estate-bottled tipples and can offer advice and tips on choosing wine. Ⓜ Mabillon, Map 12 C1 ④

Ô Château

08 00 80 11 48

100 rue de la Folie Méricourt, République   www.o-chateau.com

Olivier Magny, the 'Jamie Oliver of wine', isn't just a wine expert, he's a humorous wine expert with not a sniff of the pretentious about him. The company offers basic wine tastings from the Wine Loft near the Marais – prices start at €20 for a basic introduction, as well as wine-cheese pairings, customised tastings, and even romantic tastings atop the Eiffel Tower. Monsieur Magny also offers tours to vineyards and châteaux across France. The latter are in English and the approach is very informative and upbeat. Ⓜ Goncourt, Map 6 F4 ⑤

Spectator Sports

As one of the 'cities of the world', Paris hosts her fair share of spectacular sporting competitions; plan ahead and snare your tickets early.

Cycling

Tour de France

www.letour.fr

The Tour de France is certainly the best-known bike race in the world. The three-week journey sees competitors race through France, and occasionally neighbouring countries, over 20 one-day race stages. Look out for distinctive jerseys that the cyclists are required to wear (and are awarded after each stage): the *maillot jaune* (the yellow jersey) is worn by the leader; the *maillot vert* (green) is worn by the rider who has won the greatest number of points. Finally, the *maillot à pois rouges* (red polka dots) is awarded to the best climber on the mountainous stages. The race has a unique tradition where a rider can lead the race through their hometown or on their birthday.

Golf

Open de France

www.opendefrance.fr

The Open de France first teed off in 1906, making it the oldest professional golf tournament in Europe. With a prize fund of €4 million in 2006, it's clearly in the top echelon, with big

Professional cyclists

name players like Massy, Braid, Ballesteros and Montgomerie all having graced the winner's podium. The 2007 Open was hosted at the 7,202 yard Le Golf National, where the champion Graeme Storm managed to conquer some of the hardest holes, bunkers and water hazards in Europe.

Horse Racing

Le Prix de l'Arc de Triomphe
Bois de Boulogne

01 44 30 75 00
www.france-galop.com

One fine spring day in April of 1857, Emperor Napoleon III and his wife floated lazily down the Seine in their private yacht to watch a race in the newly constructed Hippodrome

de Longchamp, and today you can still see why this was a favourite haunt during the Second Empire. This 57 hectare horse racing facility, with four interlaced tracks of varying lengths, has retained the charm and verdure that became the subject of a few Monet paintings. Today, the biggest draw to the course is the annual Prix de l'Arc de Triomphe, the premier end-of-the-season (beginning of October) middle-distance race in Europe, featuring champions from all over the world. The track is a mile and a half long, with upward and downward sloped sections, and an exciting finish line. The winning owner bags a €1.5 million purse. Map 1 A2

Tennis

French Open
01 47 43 48 00
Stade Roland Garros, Porte de Boulogne   www.fft.fr

The French Open, also known as the *Tournoi de Roland-Garros*, is one of the four annual Grand Slam tennis tournaments. The two-week tournament takes place at the end of May, and is the premier clay court tournament in the world. Clay courts slow down the ball and allow for a higher bounce, factors which contribute to this tournament's reputation as the most physically demanding in the world. Spectators can enjoy seats in the sunshine, purchase souvenirs and, when hunger strikes, descend upon the many food tents and stalls. It is advisable to reserve tickets well in advance as it always sells out. Map 1 A3

Taking the scenic route

Spas

Scrub, steam and soak your cares away in one of the city's tranquil spas. Paris knows how to offer luxury pampering at its finest.

Anne Sémonin Atelier de Beauté
01 42 66 24 22

112 rue du Faubourg
Saint-Honoré, Champs-Élysées   www.anne-semonin.de

It's really no wonder the world's most sophisticated hotels stock Anne Sémonin products in their bathrooms. Neither is it a surprise to find the newest Anne Sémonin spa inside The Hôtel Bristol, one of Paris' famed luxury hotels. Her treatments are renowned for curing everything from blotchy skin to jetlag. Facials are a speciality; the Eye Contour Treatment helps ditch under-eye circles, while the Revitalization Treatment offers volcanic mud-induced euphoria.

Ⓜ Miromesnil, Map 4 C4 Ⓖ

Institut Guerlain
01 45 62 52 57

62 avenue des Champs-Élysées   www.guerlain.com

Synonymous with luxury, Guerlain has successfully cornered the spa market with this tiled haven on the Champs-Élysées. Designed by Andrée Putman in 2005, the spa's interior is a stylish melange of mosaic and glass. Treatments include personalised facials, make up lessons and harmonising massages, each making good use of the label's gorgeous products. Ⓜ Franklin D Roosevelt, Map 3 F2 ⓐ

L'Espace Payot

01 45 61 42 08
62 rue Pierre Charron, Champs-Élysées   www.payot.com

The swimming pool at L'Espace Payot is a technically-lit dream; slip into deep periwinkle water with its massaging pulse places and aquatic music, or simply hit the aroma-therapeutic jacuzzi. For those seeking a workout first, a personal trainer will help bend you with yoga, shape you with Pilates, and sculpt you with muscle strengthening. A hairdresser, manicurist and pedicurist are also at the ready to pamper you. And to finish? Fresh fruit juice and light snacks await you at the Payot bar. Ⓜ George V, Map 3 e3 🛇

La Bulle Kenzo

01 45 61 42 08
1 rue du Pont-Neuf, Louvre-Rivoli   www.labullekenzo.com

Situated in the fashion label's flagship store, this futuristic spa will transport you. Using coloured lights, state-of-the-art equipment and a healthy dose of humour (check out the website), this spa sets the modern standard in Paris. Choose from unique massages and facials, but if it's your mind that needs therapy then opt for 45 minutes of lying down and 'expressing yourself to your heart's content'.
Ⓜ Pont Neuf, Map 9 D3 🄲

La Sultane de Saba

01 45 00 00 40
Various Locations   www.lasultanedesaba.com

Lovers of the scents and sensibilities of the East will become fast fans of La Sultane de Saba's Parisian boutiques, modelled after a Moroccan spa with earth-tones, tiling and heavily scented air. Expect to be greeted with a mint tea and sticky

Moroccan pastry as you wait. Take a hammam, book a wax and enjoy a manicure, massage or pedicure before stocking up on the brand's lusciously scented products to take home: from a honey and ginger skin mask to a caramel and rose body scrub. Scented candles and beautifully beaded kaftans are also on sale. Products are reasonably priced from around €10 and up.

Les Bains du Marais
01 44 61 02 02

31-33 rue des Blancs-Manteaux   www.lesbainsdumarais.com

Both men and women flock to this exotic steam bath and beauty complex in the Marais, where the tired and weary can enjoy a steam bath in Moroccan-styled rooms for €35 (access to the sauna, relaxation salon and slippers, towels and dressing gown included). Make a day of it and avail yourself of the services of the in-house masseuse, beauty therapists and hairdressers before retiring to the restaurant for a refreshing mint tea. Prices range from €20 for a bikini wax to €70 for a 60 minute oil massage. Map 10 C3 **11**

Marc Dugast
01 53 10 13 30

11 rue Lobineau, Odéon   www.marcdugast.com

Marc Dugast has developed a system capable of transforming the most awkward of outsiders into stylish Parisians overnight. Morphobeauté tweaks, cleans, exfoliates and clarifies your skin; Morphobien-être kneads and massages your body; Morphorelooking sorts your rotten taste in clothes, while Morphcoiffure creates salon-perfect hair. You'll leave looking so French even the pickpockets will leave you alone. Ⓜ Mabillon, Map 12 C2 **12**

The Spa at the Four Seasons Hôtel George V

The Spa

01 49 52 70 00

Four Seasons Hôtel

George V, Champs-Élysées   www.fourseasons.com/paris

Step back in time at this classically opulent hotel. Adorned with 18th century prints, there's nothing historic about the treatments on offer; from the chocolate body scrub to the Polynesian lagoon water facial, experienced staff are employed to pamper. Luxurious to the end, there's a private VIP room with a whirlpool, sauna, steam bath, two massage beds and music stations. Hotel guests can enjoy in-room massages. Ⓜ Alma – Marceau, Map 3 E3 🔢

Shopping

PASTIS
OLIVE
ABSINTHE
DUCROS fils
TRIPLE RECTIFICATION
Alex.dre DUCROS FILS, VALENCE s/Rhône
"LIQUEUR MONT-CHRIST"
ABSINTHE
ROBETTE

Chic Shopping

From department store chic to indie boutiques, fashion-forward shoppers will be dazzled by the city's fabulous retail culture.

Ah, Paris – the City of Light, a destination for lovers, and one of the major shopping capitals of the world. Alongside romance and refinement, this city is known for its fabulous retail culture. Eager shoppers will find fancy stores selling high fashion, local shopping malls and open air markets, this is one shopping destination that aims to please. Fashion-forward shoppers will love exploring the Marais (p.162) and St-Germain (p.161), arty-types can find all manner of independent galleries in Montmartre's (p.163) lofty heights, and lovers of luxury can make their way to the chic streets of Avenue Montaigne (p.160) and Rue du Faubourg Saint-Honoré in the 1st *arrondissement* for fabulous designer boutiques.

Shop assistants are for the most part friendly and will always greet you with a *bonjour* and see you on your way with an *au revoir*. Inbetween, expect polite questions to ensure you've got the right size, colour and fit, and don't be surprised if they check on you when you're in the fitting room. So much attention can be disconcerting for those wanting a quiet browse, however simply letting

Size Wise

European sizes differ from US and UK sizes. Most clothing labels will display international sizes, if not, staff should be on hand to help.

Serpette market at Marché aux Puces de St-Ouen

them know that you're just looking usually cuts off any over-enthusiastic advances.

Prices vary, depending on the shops you go to, but Paris is by no means cheap. There are two main rates of VAT. The base rate stands at 19.6%, with a reduced rate of 5.5% that mainly applies to cultural and food products. This is already included in the prices marked. It may also be worth keeping in mind that twice yearly, in January and June, the whole city moves into official sale mode, with reductions of up to 75%.

This chapter is divided into shopping hotspots across the city, covering a selection of the best markets, malls and department stores, alongside some insider tips on the favourite streets and areas to head to for that special Parisian purchase. *Bon shopping*.

Hotspots

Parisian *quartiers* are famed for their individual personalities. Pick a neighbourhood to match your shopping mood and budget.

Avenue Montaigne

Polish up your skyscraper Louboutin heels, grab your Vuitton clutch and throw on that Marni dress – a stroll along the tree-lined avenue Montaigne is no time for haphazard fashion statements. One of the chicest spots in Paris, the avenue is home to both luxury clothing and jewellery labels alike. Check out the latest at Prada and Dior before taking a blinding peek at the goodies in Harry Winston at number 29. Break for lunch at number 41, L'Avenue cafe (a favourite with Brad Pitt, Drew Barrymore and SJP), before sipping an exquisite cocktail in the bar at the Plaza Athénée (p.51). La Maison Blanche just up the block at number 15 is a fabulous (if rather expensive) spot for dinner, with a stunning view of the Eiffel Tower.

Ⓜ Franklin D. Roosevelt, Map 3 E4 **1**

Rue de Grenelle

Stretching from the Eiffel Tower in the 7th *arrondissement* to the border of the 6th, rue de Grenelle is an interesting mix of bustling residential interest, chic boutiques and Parisian colour. Closer to the Eiffel Tower you'll find the lively pedestrian market street of rue Cler where fashionable families doing the weekly shopping mix with tourists eager to experience a little Parisian authenticity. At the other end is a clustering of great boutiques around rue du Bac and rue des Saint-Pères, including Prada, Catherine Malandrino, YSL, Diane von Furstenberg and MAC make-up. Chic department store Le Bon Marché (p.170), with its *epicerie* and glamorous fashions, is a two-minute walk.

Ⓜ Varenne, Map 8 C4 **2**

Boulevard Haussmann

It's not just the *grands magasins* of Galeries Lafayette (p.170) and Printemps (p.171) that call this 9th *arrondissement* address home. Further towards the Arc de Triomphe, homeware enthusiasts will find more than a few boutiques to hold their interest. Heading towards Opéra, there's a large branch of cosmetics chain Sephora, Zara and other independent boutiques. Ⓜ Saint-Augustin, Map 4 E1 **18**

Boulevard St-Germain

No guide of Parisian shopping streets is complete without the mention of the famed boulevard St-Germain. Perhaps it says something that – even though tourists flock here in their millions each year – it is still a space Parisians themselves are happy to claim. Near its beginnings on the border of the 7th *arrondissement* you can shop at Sonia Rykiel (175), Joseph (147) and candlemaker Dyptique (34) and enjoy an over-priced coffee at Les Deux Magots (p.236) or Café de Flore (p.235). Then, wander the narrow streets and alleys running off the boulevard and discover chic boutiques such as Miu Miu (16 rue de Grenelle). Shoe lovers will be in awe along rue de Rennes, rue de Cherche-Midi and rue de Grenelle. Ⓜ Odéon, Map 12 D2 **3**

Rue Charlot & Rue de Poitou

You can barely walk a metre along these two streets in the *haut* Marais without discovering yet another boutique whose patrons clearly worship at the altar of design. Justifiably labelled 'the chicest addresses in the Marais', expect to encounter über-styled locals and fashionable tourists staying at Hôtel du Petit Moulin (29/31, Rue de Poitou). Pick up a floral-inspired bag from designer Dominique Picquier's self-named space, or peruse the eclectic mix of Scandinavian antiques and paintings at Anders' Hut. And all this against a backdrop of ancient streets. Ⓜ Filles du Calvaire, Map 10 C2 **4**

Rue du Roi de Sicile, Rue des Francs Bourgeois & Rue des Rosiers

This intersecting triangle of streets in the heart of the Marais – the city's original Jewish neighbourhood – reveals all you'll need to know about what is one of the hippest quarters in Paris. On rue des Rosiers you'll find a multitude of Jewish *epiceries*, bakeries, falafel outposts and, among them, the avant-garde boutique L'Eclaireur: adventurous and knowledgeable fashion types come here for the great collection of women's and men's brands. Next, take a stroll along Roi du Sicile for edgy street duds, or head to rue des Franc Bourgeois to discover a mix of well-known and boutique-name brands. Recognised as the heart of the city's gay district, men's fashion features highly. Once night descends, grab a drink at The Lizard Lounge (18 rue Bourg-Tibourg, 01 42 72 81 34), just off rue du Roi de Sicile. There's a great, vibrant scene in the Marais, and it's one of the few areas of Paris open on a Sunday. Ⓜ Saint-Paul, Map 10 C4 **5**

Rue Etienne Marcel, Rue Montorgueil & Rue Montmartre

Et Vous, Diesel, 58M, Barbara Bui, Maje… the list of hot boutiques lining rue Etienne Marcel and rue Montmartre extends as a who's who of the chic-street fashion world. Around the corner on rue Montorgueil discover one of the oldest market streets in Paris, now an interesting mix of old and new: from the horse meat butcher at number 72 to the minimalist cafe, Santi, at number 49. Ⓜ Étienne Marcel, Map 9 E1 **6**

Rue Lepic & Rue des Abbesses

In the shadow of Sacré-Cœur, away from the tourist hordes, discover romantic Paris in the hilly, narrow streets of Montmartre. A favoured location of the bohemian and artistic sets, this vibrant area has galleries, boho boutiques, relaxed bars and a colourful Sunday street market. Finish shopping and explore the last vineyard in Paris before taking in the Moulin de la Galette – the windmill once painted by Renoir.
Ⓜ Abbesses, Map 2 B2 **7**

Rue-St-Louis-en-l'Île

In one of the oldest areas of Paris, the main street running the length of the Île Saint-Louis provides an amazingly atmospheric backdrop to the selection of gourmet food shops, gift shops, art galleries and restaurants found here. The cobbled street is especially beautiful in winter. Stop at the beautiful La Charlotte en l'Île at number 24 (01 47 54 25 83) for tea and cake, or stop at Berthillon at number 31 (01 43 54 31 61) for a luscious scoop of ice-cream. Ⓜ Pont Marie, Map 13 B2 **8**

Markets

From antique finds to delectable gourmet treats, browsing the city's myriad markets is an experience not to be missed.

Carreau du Temple

Rue Eugene-Spuller & rue du Petit-Thouars, République

A 19th century covered market hall, the Carreau du Temple provides a grand backdrop to what is essentially a specialist clothing market. Fans of leather clothing flock here to find the garment of their dreams, choosing everything from fitted leather pants to stylish blouses. The market is positioned within the heart of the *quartier* Sentier, the city's original garment district, so there's plenty more boutiques to browse nearby once you've scouted the best of the clothing on offer.

Ⓜ Temple, Map 10 D1 **9**

Market Research

For a full list of markets in each of the city's 20 *arrondissements* go to www. paris.fr and click the link 'Les Marché Parisiens'.

Bouquinistes

Pont Neuf, The Seine

Something between a market and an open-air collection of like-minded sales people, the bouquinistes stalls lining the Seine around Pont Neuf provide a wonderful shopping experience for those with a love for second-hand books, antique posters and quirky paper collectibles. **Ⓜ** Pont Neuf, Map 9 D4 **10**

Marché aux Puces de St-Ouen

Marché aux Puces de St-Ouen

Porte de Clignancourt, St-Ouen

With some 1,000 fashion vendors and more than 2,500 antique and second-hand bric-a-brac stores, this market provides a universe of flea-market finds for savvy shoppers. The combination of shouting vendors, shrewd art dealers and excited visitors makes wandering the many aisles a great experience, though the onslaught of tourist buses means prices have skyrocketed, and this is a pickpocket's paradise so be very careful. Ⓜ Porte de Clignancourt

Marché de Vanves

Ave Marc Sangnier & ave George Lafenestre, Malakoff

The only flea market inside the city limits, Marché de Vanves specialises in small objets d'art, textiles, great second-hand clothing and handbags. Being more local than Marché aux Puces de St-Ouen means foragers can still find some fantastic finds at really good prices. The atmosphere is very relaxed, as are the opening hours – many vendors pack up at lunchtime, so get there early. Ⓜ Porte de Vanves, Map 1 B4

Marché des Batignolles

Terre-plein des Batignolles, Batignolles

Newer and more intimate than the organic market on boulevard Raspail, this organic produce market attracts foodies from across Paris. Recommendations include the fruit and veg from the house of Giboulot, cheeses from La Table du Roy, pastries from the stand Gustalin, and crème fraîche brought from Normandy by Henri Martin. Ⓜ Rome, Map 1 C1

Marché Mouffetard

Rue Mouffetard, Mouffetard

Rue Mouffetard is universally considered one of the most ancient and lively of all Parisian streets. Sunday mornings are particularly colourful, with the street's produce market in full swing and hordes of funky Parisians brunching and chatting up a storm. Bars, too, are worth a visit: try The 5th Bar or Le Verre a Pied before throwing back some oysters at L'Huitre et Demie. Ⓜ Censier Daubenton, Map 15 C1 **11**

Marché Raspail

Cnr rue de Rennes & rue du Cherche-Midi, Montparnasse

One of the most well-known food markets in Paris, Marché Raspail attracts French celebs, gastro tourists and local gourmands. Though much of the produce is exceptional, there are some especially great vendors to look out for; try the comté from the fromagerie Sumière, pick up some fruit and veg at Conard and grab sweet and savoury nibbles from 'Madame Annie'. Ⓜ Rennes, Map 11 F3 **12**

Rue Poncelet

Rue Poncelet, Etoile

Between the German patisserie, Stubli, the gourmet hot dog stand of Epicurya, and the cool art deco surrounds of Le Dada café, rue Poncelet is precisely the type of permanent, open-air market street which attracts food-focused locals and tourists alike. The beautiful fruits and cakes, the scent of fresh-cooked paella, and the lively chat and bustling market-day feel will certainly stimulate your senses. Ⓜ Ternes, Map 1 B2

Malls & Department Stores

Elegance and history combine in the *grands magasins* of Paris, where the architecture is as stunning as the wares waiting to be discovered.

Carrousel du Louvre

01 43 16 47 10
Musée du Louvre
www.louvre.fr

It seems almost sacrilegious to consider housing a shopping complex in the basement of one of the world's greatest museums, but that is exactly what has happened. There are 50 boutiques here specialising in fashion, music, beauty, games and hobbies, alongside restaurants, parking and an exhibition space. Being part of the Louvre, services here are fantastic, encompassing wheelchair and pram hire, postal services, baggage storage and information booths in multiple languages. Ⓜ Louvre Rivoli, Map 9 B2 🔢

Citadium

01 55 31 74 00
50-56 rue Caumartin, Opéra
www.citadium.com

Tucked behind Printemps and Galeries Lafayette in the 9th, Citadium is a four-storey paradise for lovers of street and sport fashion. From Vans and Converse to Le Coq Sportif and Puma, Citadium safely covers every conceivable mainstream urban fashion statement. The store runs regular brand promotions on the ground-floor, alongside the occasional concert. A word of warning: the weekend can bring long queues as youthful shoppers snap up the latest sneakers or Carhartt pants. Ⓜ Havre-Caumartin, Map 1 C2

Clockwise from top left: Marché aux Puces de St-Ouen, fresh seafood, Galeries Lafayette

Galeries Lafayette

01 42 82 34 56

40 blvd Haussmann, Opéra   www.galerieslafayette.com

Of all the city's department stores, 'les Galeries' attracts the largest number of tourists. Spread across multiple buildings, the most stunning architecturally is the main building, with it's central atrium that extends the full seven storeys, topped by a mosaic glass dome. Here you'll find cosmetics, hoisery plus accessories, ladies and childrens fashion. In summer, head to the rooftop cafe and terrace for the decent food and stunning view. It's neighbouring sections include menswear, food, and home decor. Underground parking is available but public transport access is excellent and right outside. There's an English-speaking welcome service on the ground floor, free shopping advice service and clothing alterations can be made for a small fee. Ⓜ Chaussée d'Antin La Fayette, Map 5 A1 **14**

Le Bon Marché

01 44 39 80 00

24 rue de Sèvres, St-Germain des Prés   www.lebonmarche.fr

Smaller and more intimate than either Galeries Lafayette or Printemps, Le Bon Marché exudes an atmosphere of genteel chic. The myriad luxury brand counters account for all the major fashion players, from Balenciaga and Burberry, to Galliano and Gaultier. A passageway from the main floor leads to more wallet-friendly labels such as Paul & Joe and Zadig & Voltaire. Menswear, toys, high-end women's shoes, handbags, lingerie and perfume all feature too. Next door, La Grande Epicerie, the famed food section, sells exotic fruits, delicious pastries and breads, international foods and decadent ready-made meals. Ⓜ Sèvres Babylone, Map 11 E2 **15**

Les Forums des Halles

01 44 76 96 56
www.forumdeshalles.com

101 Porte Berger, Beaubourg

Formerly the city's main food market, this combined indoor and outdoor mall now boasts a 50 metre pool, gardens, two cinemas, 24 hour parking and 19 restaurants. Shoppers will find an enormous range of shops specialising in everything from fashion, homeware and beauty to jewellery, electronics, optics and games. The cinemas and some restaurants are open Sundays. As for clientele, this has become a central meeting point for the city's youth. The atmosphere is vibrant if the area a little grubby. Les Halles does attract some unsavoury elements so beware of pickpockets and avoid late-night visits. Ⓜ Châtelet-Les Halles, Map 9 F2 **16**

Printemps

01 42 82 57 87
www.printemps.com

64 blvd Haussmann, Opéra

Printemps is one of the main centres for Parisian fashion; the department store is incredibly sleek (with prices to match) and includes one of the largest beauty floors in the world. Laid out over three buildings – Printemps men, fashion, and home – its hallmark is the amazing art nouveau glass cupola in the main fashion store. Choice is limitless, as are services. Alongside a free image and consultancy service, parents can also make use of a free short-stay nursery. Foodwise, Printemps excels. There is a Ladurée cafe, a boulangerie concept created by Alain Ducasse, an organic restaurant in the beauty department, sushi on the fashion floor, a wine bar designed by Paul Smith, and a sublime brasserie under the cupola of the main building. Ⓜ Havre-Caumartin, Map 4 F1 **17**

Where To Go For…

Art

Alongside food and fashion, it is art that makes up the third piece in the Holy Trinity of Parisian passions. From street portrait sketchers along the Seine and amateur painters in the place du Tertre, to international artists displaying in galleries, finding pieces to your taste and budget is easy, once you've managed to narrow down the vast array of choice. For the best atmosphere visit the city's known art quarters, including St-Germain des Prés in the 6th (www.artsaintgermaindespres.com) and Montmartre in the 18th (www.art-montmartre.com). For a comprehensive overview of exhibitions, artists, photographers and galleries, log onto www.paris-art.com. Those seeking advice should try art buyers such as Arzao (06 23 15 42 56), a company specialising in personalised shopping trips and auction visits.

French-Look Fashion

Local brands are renowned for their flattering cuts, body-skimming fabrics and softly neutral colour palettes. All can be found in various stores throughout the city. Comptoir des Cotonniers (33 rue des Francs-Bourgeois, 4th) is great value for trend buying, offering better quality than high street buys but less expensive than designer gear. Et Vous (69 rue de Rennes, 6th), Vanessa Bruno (25 rue St Sulpice, 6th) and Zadig & Voltaire (42 rue des Francs Bourgeois, 4th) are all slightly more expensive, however the cuts, quality and styles justify the price tags: if you want that certain *je ne sais quoi*, this is where to get it. Isabel Marant (16 rue Charonne, 11th) – famed for her drapey cuts – and Barbara Bui (23 rue Etienne

Marcel, 2nd) are both one more step up the price ladder. At Antik Batik (18 rue de Turenne, 2nd) you'll find a complete style change; this brand is renowned for its Indian-inspired, beaded and glittery fabrics cut in beautifully modern pieces. For men, start at APC (4 rue de Fleurus, 6th) for well-cut basics in quality fabrics. Agnès B Homme (6 rue du Jour, 1st), also does a good job of outfitting those seeking that well-cut, casual Euro vibe. Father & Sons (51 avenue Général Leclerc, 14th) and Melchior (15 rue Vieille du Temple, 4th) are both a little more mainstream, but are well-priced and good choices for casual shirts and jackets that could go from work to weekend. And then there's Jack Henry (1 rue Montmartre, 1st): cuts are slim and edgy.

Gourmet Goods

Paris is a gourmet paradise, hosting an endless array of fine food stores, each more fantastic than the last. For luscious, unpasteurised cheeses head to the 7th where you'll find Marie Ann Cantin (12 rue Champ de Mars), for camembert and certain rare offerings try Alléosse in the 17th (13 rue Poncelet). Discover rich chocolate truffles with Jean-Paul Hevin (23bis avenue de la Motte Picquet, 15th), Patrick Roger (108 boulevard St-Germain, 6th) and La Maison du Chocolat (19 rue Sèvres, 7th), or indulge in fabulously rich desserts at Pierre Hermé (72 rue Bonaparte) in the 6th. Famously decadent gourmet superstores, La Grande Epicerie (Le Bon Marché, p.170) in the 7th, Fauchon (26-30) and Hédiard (21), both at place de la Madeleine in the 8th, sell an enormous range of delicious edibles and have in-house tea salons.

Haute Vintage Clothing

With its six stores clustered in the one street in the 16th, Reciproque (95 rue de la pompe, 16th) is the first port of call for men and women seeking luxury label vintage buys. Le Mouton à Cinq Pattes (138 Boulevard St-Germain, 6th) is another vintage chain with multiple outlets selling a great selection of second-hand designer labels. A great indie find is Quidam de Revel (24 rue Poitou) in the 3rd, offering a hand-picked selection from such designers as YSL, Cardin and Hermès, and with jewellery from Georg Jensen among others. Trend store Kiliwatch (64 rue Tiquetonne) in the 2nd falls somewhere between second-hand and vintage. The super hip boutique just off rue Etienne Marcel sells new trend brands, but the largest portion of the store is given over to 'vintage' pieces.

Lingerie

Lingerie is big business in the city of romance. For something fashionable and affordable, lingerie chains Etam (60 rue de Rennes, 6th) and Princesse Tam-Tam (52 Boulevard St-Michel, 6th) house a great range of options; everything from peek-a-boo lace to the more sensible and sturdy. For a 1950s aesthetic head to one of the city's Fifi Chachnil boutiques (231 rue St Honoré, 1st) where you'll find fluffy, feminine designs in a boudoir-style setting. High-end, luxury boutiques Sabbia Rosa (73 rue des Sts-Pères) in the 7th, Fanny Liautard (13 rue St-Florentin) in the 8th, and Alice Cadolle (4 rue Cambon, 1st) will hand-make lingerie in specific styles and colours for enthusiastic clients. Of these, however, it is Cadolle that is justifiably the most well-known; Marguerite

Cadolle measured lingerie for Mata Hari in the 1920s and her granddaughter, Poupie, continues to run the business today. Bras can cost up to €300 and boned corsets twice as much. Grandiva (01 46 22 00 44) in the 7th specialises in luxury lingerie for full-figured women, taking private appointments two days a week.

Perfumes & Cosmetics

In a city where even a Sunday morning visit to the *boulangerie* requires an acceptable level of dress and styling, the beauty industry is correspondingly large in size and presence. Nothing is too specialised: Frank Vidoff, (01 42 22 66 33) runs a salon in the 7th *arrondissement* dedicated to the art of blonde colouring. Pedicurist Bastien Gonzales, at Hotel Costes (239 rue St Honoré, 01 42 44 50 00) in the 1st, is sought-out by foot fetishists for his amazing pedicure treatments and self-named product line (book well in advance).

Specialist beauty superstore Marionnaud (www.marionnaud. fr) is dotted all over the city and is a great place to seek out a wide selection of well-known brands, as is Sephora's megastore at number 70 on the Champs Elysées. For specialist perfumes try Editions de Parfums Frédéric Malle (37 rue de Grenelle, 7th) and Annick Goutal (16 rue de Bellechasse). By Terry (36 Galerie Véro-Dodat, 1st), and Guerlain (68 avenue des Champs Elysées, 8th) are some of the city's best make up brands, while L'Occitane (55 rue St-Louis-en-l'Île, 4th) is a favourite for lotions and potions for the skin and scented products for the home. If you're short on time, most of the above have outlets in the major department stores (p.168).

Spécialités
de Montag

Going Out

FONDUE SAVOY
aux 3 fromag
Savoyarde 3 cheeses "fo

14,80 €

DUE au chèvre
lk cheese "fondue"
14,80 €

Bonne Soirée

No matter what your party predilection, Paris has something to meet your needs, from fashionable bars to vibrant clubs where you can dance from dusk till dawn.

Paris is one city where 'going out' is all about eating out. Foodies travel from all corners of the globe to dine in this epicurean magnet: as Julia Child brought French cuisine into the home during the 1960s, the world's fascination with gastronomy increased the spotlight on Paris' restaurants.

Today the array of choice is mind-boggling. Taste the talent of top-rated chefs such as Alain Ducasse, Joel Robuchon, Pierre Gagnaire, and Hélène Darroze, visit the city's two Chinatowns (one at place d'Italie and the other around Belleville), join the new brunch trend, or make like a local with a *formule*, a fixed-price menu made up of a combination of an *entrée*, *plat* (main course) and a dessert. Dress well and easily make the transition from dinner date to night on the town. As you'll soon discover, the only institution more established than the neighbourhood bistro is the neighbourhood bar. *Santé*.

Local Cuisine

Food products must follow strict standards in order to be considered an authentic representation of one of the more than 400 regions and receive an AOC (Appellation d'Origine Contrôlée) certification. The restaurant L'AOC (p.210) uses only endorsed ingredients in their expert cuisine, and is a not-to-be-missed opportunity to explore France's abundant styles.

Neighbouring Germany has heavily flavoured the dishes of the Alsace-Lorraine region, as discovered in the hearty sausages and sauerkraut paired with floral rieslings and gewurztraminers. Normandy excels with scallops and mussels, in addition to apple products like cider, calvados and tarte normande. Sweet *crêpes* and savoury buckwheat *galettes* originate from Brittany; Breizh Café (p.190) serves the real thing made from organic grains. This area and the Marennes-Oléron basin on the Atlantic coast are the oyster capitals; for a taste of the freshest *fines de claires* in town, Huîtriere Régis (p.237) stands out. The Périgord region further south is home to Cognac and all things *canard*.

In Bordeaux, specialities of roasted lamb and steaks with *bordelaise* sauce blend beautifully with the district's stellar wines, while central France hosts the Champagne, Bourgogne and Loire Valley regions, boasting spectacular vineyards and fragrant melons, strawberries, cherries, and blackcurrants for kir and other liqueurs. Goat's cheese and *andouille* sausage are traditions of the Loire; dijon mustard, *escargots* and the buttery *epoisses* cheese reign in Bourgogne. The Alpine area is home to the monks of Chartreuse, whose liqueur is a 400-year-old secret recipe made from 130 herbs. Switzerland's influence is noted too with the cheese *raclettes* and fondues; Les Fromages de Pierre (148 ave Félix Faure, 15th, 01 45 54 12 26) is a cheese lover's paradise showcasing traditional variations. The gastronomic city of Lyon is particularly known for its garlicky pepper sausage and hearty Rhône Valley cuisine; Aux Lyonnais (32, rue St Marc, 01 42 96 65 04) in the 2nd offers fine examples under the helm of Ducasse. The Mediterranean spirit of Provence is embodied through the lush vegetables, garlic, lavender, olive oil, and seafood which perfectly complement the region's spicy wines and *pastis apéritif*. *Ratatouille* and *bouillabaisse* stews as well as *pissaladière*, Nice's pizza-like tart with onions, anchovies and olives, are typical dishes. The menu at Chez Janou (p.191) features Provençal interpretations in a sunny, laid-back setting.

Cafes, Bistros & Brasseries

It can be difficult for a newcomer to know what to expect from each of Paris' different types of dining establishments. The distinctions generally relate to the scope of food and the time of day (and atmosphere) in which it is served. *Cafés* have a casual ambience and offer inexpensive cold sandwiches and salads. Historically a *bistro* serves a small selection of simple, hot meals at lunchtime and, in some instances, at dinner: The term *bistro*, Russian for 'quick', was popularised in 1814 when the Cossacks occupying Paris would pound on the bar's zinc countertop and shout 'bistro' to command speedy service. In the past a *brasserie*, French for 'brewery', made its own beer and served food from the Alsace region. Over time it has come to mean a large, beautifully decorated place with a bustling ambience serving traditional French cuisine during the day and often late into the night. A restaurant, on the other hand, usually closes mid-afternoon and serves meals at a more leisurely pace.

Drinking

Drinking alcohol is closely intertwined with socialising and meals in France, where the legal drinking age is 16. In restaurants a bottle of wine begins around €17, while an individual glass or a draft beer (*un pression*) is at least €5. Mixed drinks are pricier with a €10 minimum depending on the venue. Cocktail bars are a staple of the party scene, ranging from the legendary Harry's Bar (p.224) to the ephemeral cool of the Hôtel Costes (p.225). France is an oenophile's paradise; Willi's Wine Bar (p.226) and the tasting room inside the Lavinia (3 blvd de la Madeleine, 1st, 01 42 97 20 20) wine shop are notable for their vast selections.

Timings & Tipping

Though you will find some eateries serving all hours, most close at around 14:30, reopening at about 19:30 for supper. Locals typically dine around 21:00 or 22:00 (most restaurants seat diners until 22:00 during the week and 23:30 on weekends). Sunday and Monday serve as the 'weekend', and many eateries close or run reduced hours. Some also choose to join the masses on summer vacation, shutting shop

The Yellow Star

The little yellow star highlights venues that merit extra praise. It could be the atmosphere, the food, the cocktails, the music or the crowd, but whatever the reason, any review that you see with the star attached is somewhere considered a bit special.

in July and August. As far as tipping goes, a service charge of about 15% (which goes to the employer) and the standard value-added tax (VAT) rate of 19.6% are built into the price of each menu item. As a token of appreciation, €1 following a round of drinks at a cafe, or 10% in a restaurant will be appreciated but is not expected.

Vegetarian Food

France has not traditionally been known for its vegetarian-friendly fare, but as more restaurants focus on providing health-conscious options it's becoming much easier to dine meat-free. French *bistros* can become monotonous after a dozen *chèvre* salads, though the city's rich assortment of ethnic spots and fusion locales provides tasty alternatives. Korean restaurant L'Arbre du Sel (p.246) has a daily vegetarian *formule* and Living B'Art (p.230) uses free-trade and equitable commerce ingredients in their hearty dishes. There are also 100% vegetarian or vegan joints such as La Victoire Suprême du Cœur (p.223), where the fresh creations are all non-GMO.

Restaurant Listing Structure

To review every eating and drinking venue in Paris would be a lifetime's work and would fill countless volumes, so this Going Out section presents a cross section of the city's recommended outlets. Restaurants have been independently reviewed, categorised by cuisine, and are listed in alphabetical order. If any review has led you astray, or your favourite venue is missing from these pages, drop us a line at info@explorerpublishing.com.

Typical eating and drinking options in Paris

Beaubourg, The Marais & Bastille

The destination of choice for anyone seeking a great night out, Paris' historic heart offers chic restaurants, cosy cafes and risqué clubs with no holds barred.

Since Parisians generally abide by a live-and-let-live policy, the gay community has found Paris to be a great place to live, love, and proudly fly their flag. Le Marais, in the 3rd and 4th *arrondissements*, is the epicentre of the gay community. You can find anything from a cosy corner bar or stylish lounge, to a sleazy sex bar where you can fulfil your every fantasy and the word 'taboo' doesn't translate. That said there are also plenty of good times to be had by the straight crowd.

Venue Finder

Cafes

Le Loir dans la Théière

3 rue des Rosiers   01 42 72 90 61

Curl up in one of the many mismatched chairs, sip a steaming
mug of jasmine tea and discuss life with the artistic folk who
have made this inexpensive, cosy joint an institution in the
Marais. An old-fashioned sideboard displays the freshly baked
strawberry tarts and apple crumbles, and a small menu offers
light salad and omelette lunch options. Laptops forbidden.

Ⓜ Saint-Paul, Map 10 C4 **1**

Mariages Frères

30 rue du Bourg-Tibourg   01 42 72 28 11

The Mariage family has served imported spices and tea to
French royalty since the 18th century. Today, commoners
can enjoy the ceremonial art of afternoon tea in this beautiful

Beaubourg, The Marais & Bastille

Marais salon, where hundreds of exotic *mélanges* are waiting to be discovered alongside light lunches and luscious desserts. The salon includes a boutique selling take home tins of the fragrant blends. Ⓜ Hôtel de Ville, Map 10 B4 **2**

Restaurants

404   Moroccan
69 rue des Gravilliers   01 42 74 57 81

This magical and mysterious late-night rendezvous is a sensual feast; dramatic lights cast scattered shadows over 16th century cobbled walls and snugly placed tabletops, leading to a private, candlelit courtyard. Dig in to fragrant couscous, and tagines filled with grilled meats and vegetables served in handmade pottery by gracious waiters. This has been a favoured haunt for fashionistas and media crowds for 20 years. Ⓜ Arts et Métiers, Map 10 B1 **3**

Breizh Café   French
109 rue Vieille du Temple   01 42 72 13 77

Paris' widespread crêpe stands can in no way compare to what is on offer at this inexpensive, family-friendly Breton bistro. Delicate, lacy *crêpes* (sweet) and *galettes* (savoury) of organic buckwheat are filled hot off the griddle and served on the region's rustic pottery. Choose from over 15 artisanal ciders or calvados to accompany your meal. Enjoy the award-winning Tsarkaya oysters here which are a rare find from the region.

Ⓜ Saint-Sébastien Froissart, Map 10 D2 **4**

Calle 24

Latin American

13 rue Beautreillis

01 42 72 38 34

Hot Havana rhythms and ripe Caribbean cuisine add up to a spicy night at Calle 24, a couple of blocks from Bastille. Percussion-laden mambo provides a sexy aural backdrop to stone walls displaying rotating collections of Cuban artists, while chef Mechy presents the flavours of his Havana hometown through tasty tapas, hot plates and desserts. The mojitos are fab. Ⓜ Bastille, Map 13 D1 **5**

Chez Janou

French

2 rue Roger Verlomme

01 42 72 28 41

Around the corner from place des Vosges, Chez Janou recalls the best of Provence with its more than 80 types of pastis and wide range of quality, affordable Rhône Valley wines. Oh, and that's not forgetting the Mediterranean cuisine. Since 1912 this neighbourhood favourite has attracted regulars with Provençal-influenced dishes such as chilled ratatouille. The garden-like terrace is lovely. Ⓜ Chemin Vert, Map 10 E4 **6**

Georges

International

19 rue Beaubourg

01 44 78 47 99

On the sixth floor of the Centre Pompidou, Georges is a Thierry Costes hotspot offering an eye-popping view of the city's skyline and decor to match; the futuristic, post-modern design by Dominique Jacob and Brendan McFarlane takes it cues from the museum's industrial architecture, with aluminium pods housing the kitchen and VIP room. Asian-accented cuisine is served by model-sexy waiting staff. Ⓜ Rambuteau, Map 10 A2 **7**

Guillaume

International

32 rue de Picardie

01 44 54 20 60

The restaurant Guillaume is truly a collaborative effort by the family and friends of its down-to-earth namesake: art from his mother's house, dining tables from his aunt's, and friends who decorated the walls and are proud to serve Belgian Chef Xavier Thierry's *cuisine du monde*. Inventive without being pretentious, enjoy seasonal dishes like sea bass ceviche with peaches. Reservations recommended. Ⓜ Temple, Map 10 D1 🔳

Micky's Deli

Deli

23bis rue des Rosiers

01 48 04 79 31

For those times when nothing but hot pastrami on rye will do. Serving kosher cuisine under orthodox rabbinic supervision, this inexpensive family-oriented Jewish deli is located in the Marais' historic heart. Enjoy its New York deli atmosphere while eating piled-high bagels, or choose the 'Micky', an American-style burger with pastrami. Closed Friday evening and Saturday. Ⓜ Saint-Paul, Map 10 C4 🔳

La Pirada

Spanish

7 rue de la Lappe

01 47 00 73 61

The cheerful, mosaic-tiled restaurant serves up spicy and saucy plates to a lively dining crowd. Capturing the sociable spirit of the sun-drenched Iberian culture, well-priced tapas are a specialty of this late-night (05:00 on weekends) spot. Try Iberico ham, manchego cheese, or a luscious paella, washed down with sangria or a rich rioja. Ⓜ Bastille, Map 1 E3

Unico

Unico

15 rue Paul Bert

Argentinean

01 43 67 68 08

Two Argentinean-born residents of Paris, an architect and a photographer, have created this stylish new Bastille hotspot frequented by the in-crowd. The 70s spirit of this former butcher's shop is preserved through the retro counter, umber wall tiles and harvest gold pendant lamps, while the slabs of beef hanging on the meat rack are an icon of the space's prior life. Food fans have been raving about the flavourful pampas beef cooked in a charcoal grill imported from Argentina, especially the lomo with spicy chimichurri sauce and the stuffed empanadas accompanied by a regional malbec wine. The filling, upscale dinner is best appreciated at the community dining table, and advance reservations for this non-smoking restaurant are a must. Open midday to 14:30, and 20:00 to 22:30. Closed Sunday and Monday.

Ⓜ Faidherbe Chaligny, Map 1 E3

Bars

Andy Wahloo

69 rue Gravilliers   01 42 71 20 38

Overturned paint can seats, mismatched tables, ornate
chandeliers, lanterns, bottles and tins adorn the walls of
this creatively kitsch bar, attracting a fashionable crowd
enamoured by the cocktails and ambient Arabic Rai music.
When warm weather hits, everyone fights for space out in the
back terrace for an almost authentic summer escape. This is a
Moroccan pop art journey. ⓜ Arts et Métiers, Map 10 A1 **10**

Bar Fleur's

3 rue Tournelles   01 42 71 04 51

Day or night, satisfy all your senses at this florist-cum-
watering-hole, where sweet-scented blooms frame a sleek
bar serving luscious champagne and vodka cocktails.
Traditional, or infused with flower essences, the drinks are
the perfect complement to the bright and beautiful shop,
complete with monthly art exhibitions by local artists. A truly
unique concept. ⓜ Bastille, Map 13 E1 **11**

La Belle Hortense

31 rue Vieille du Temple   01 48 04 71 60

Capitalising on two of the most important pastimes in Paris
(wine and literature) is La Belle Hortense, where the clever
owner realised how well good drinks and good books
combine. The small bar with its multi-language library feels
like a second home, while the front room is a lively spot to

Legrand Filles et Fils

meet-and-greet. The personable bar tender keeps glasses full and beautiful little canapes coming. Beyond charming, it's Paris at its best. Ⓜ Saint-Paul, Map p.10 C4 **12**

Legrand Filles et Fils

1 rue de la Banque   01 4 26 07 12

This 120-year old épicerie-cum-wine store received a new lease on life in 2000, when new owners both restored and expanded the space to encompass an intimate wine bar. Snug alongside Galerie Vivienne (a beautiful pedestrian arcade designed in 1823), the wine bar serves up nibbly platters alongside wines by the glass or bottle. Sip until 19:00, when the bar turns classroom. Ⓜ Bourse, Map 5 D4 **13**

Le Murano

13 blvd du Temple   01 42 71 20 00

With its leather couches and sizzling fire, the super sleek,
all-white lobby of this urban resort sets it apart from the
pack. Pull up a colourful stool to the long bar where you can
sample delicious cocktails and 100 different types of vodka
from test tubes. The restaurant is impressive and both staff
and clientele are chic and pleasantly unpretentious.

Ⓜ Filles du Calvaire, Map 10 E1 **14**

La Perle

78 rue Vieille du Temple   01 42 72 69 93

Whether it's the name that established itself as a precious
locale, or rumours that bartenders spike drinks with absinthe,
La Perle is a hotspot attracting wearers of interesting and
unusual fashion looks. Make your way early down this cobblestoned street if you hope to score a decent vantage point to
scope out the tragically trendy.

Ⓜ Saint-Sébastien Froissart, Map 10 C3 **15**

Wini June

16 rue Dupetit-Thouars   01 44 61 76 41

Classy chic meets Empirical charm in this tiny gem of a wine
bar. Walk into a wonderland and enjoy the eclectic antique
furniture, soft candlelight, and beautiful flowers accenting
the tables. Wine is poured in Baccarat glassware, and luscious
canapes are offered early evenings. Though more expensive
than your average bar, the attention to detail warrants it.

Ⓜ Temple, Map 6 D4 **16**

Gay & Lesbian

3W Kafé

8 rue des Ecouffes   01 48 87 39 26

In place of one of Paris' most notorious lesbian bars, Les
Scandaleuse, comes 3W – 'women with women'. Modern,
chic, and feminine, the pretty purple bar, comfy red couches
draws an upmarket clientele. There is a basement with a DJ
and regular theme nights, including fortune-telling every
Monday, and singles night the first Thursday of the month.

Ⓜ Saint-Paul, Map 10 C4 **17**

Cox

15 rue des Archives   01 42 72 08 00

As the trendification of the Marais continues, and the lines
between gay and straight blur, the subtly named Cox is
standing strong as exclusively gay. The tiny inside bar is
standing-room-only during Happy Hour, and the sea of big,
burly men overflows onto the pavement. Notorious for its
decor, Cox undergoes a complete makeover and changes its
look each season. Ⓜ Hôtel de Ville, Map 10 B3 **18**

Le CUD

12 rue des Haudriettes   01 42 77 44 12

If you haven't already been swept off your feet, retreat to Le
CUD with hope in your heart. The tiny first floor bar offers a
reprieve from the real action down below: descend the spiral
staircase, checking in whatever amount of clothing you wish
before entering this wall-to-wall den of nocturnal partiers

and prowlers. The stone caves, with two bars, can make you lose all track of time as you dance the night away. The exclusively gay bar allows accompanied women.
Ⓜ Rambuteau, Map 10 B2 **19**

PM Café

20 rue du Plâtre   01 42 72 43 70

Offering a reprieve from the madness of the Marais is this little gem of a cafe: relax among the lavish gold and red velvet decor with a coffee, milkshake, or delectable cocktail. Friendly staff and clientele lend this the feeling of a true neighbourhood establishment. Though predominantly gay, all are welcome. Things pick up in the evenings, especially on the weekends and for special soirees.
Ⓜ Hôtel de Ville, Map 10 B3 **20**

Raidd

23 rue du Temple   01 48 87 80 25

This is a one-of-a-kind temple to campdom. Where else are drinks served by the half-naked ensemble of the Village People, while naked men shower as you dance to a lip-syncing drag queen, before descending to the 100% men, 100% sex basement? Raidd is known for going above and beyond the call of the party gods, but that's what makes it the liveliest joint this side of boystown. The bartenders are painfully good looking and woo everyone that utters the word 'cocktail.' Girls are welcome upstairs, but the basement is strictly men only. Ⓜ Hôtel de Ville, Map 10 A3 **21**

Kebab shop in The Marais

GRANDE SALLE
À
L'ÉTAGE

SANDWICH
GREC
4.50€

ASSIETTE GRECQUE
6.00€
SUPER ASSIETTE
7.50€
BOISSONS
À EMPORTER
1,60€

PENTADAKTYLOS

prix en €

The Champs-Élysées

Surrounded by slick lounges, rooftop terraces and vibrant clubs pounding out the hottest beats, this is where the super stylish come to play.

The Champs-Élysées has the market on über-glam, Asian theme, bordello style, and super select clubs where the beautiful people play.

Though lovers of stylish, high-end restaurants will certainly find their culinary home by the Champs, it is visiting night owls who will really fall in love with the city's most famed boulevard: from campy fun at Queen, to a glam night at Neo, the area is the beating heart of Paris' club scene.

The most select clubs don't charge a cover, but you can expect to pay between €10 and €20 at some others for entrance; this sometimes includes a drink ticket.

Venue Finder

Cafes	La Galerie des Gobelins	p.201
American	⭐ PDG	p.203
Arabic/Lebanese	Noura	p.202
Contemporary	Mood	p.202
French	⭐ Alain Ducasse au Plaza Athénée	p.201
French	Taillevent	p.204
Indian	Ratn	p.203
International	Pershing Hall	p.203
Steakhouses	⭐ Le Relais de l'Entrecote	p.204

Cafes

La Galerie des Gobelins

25 ave Montaigne   01 53 67 66 00

Leagues ahead of your everyday cafe, this is undeniably Paris'
most plush and memorable spot for afternoon tea, with
its sterling silver teapots, dainty petits-fours and twinkling
harp music. Soak up the old-fashioned glamour of the Plaza
Athénée and watch the couture-clad beauties sashay around
the Louis XVI *fauteuils*. Open daily 08:00 to 01:00.

Ⓜ Alma – Marceau, Map 3 F4 **22**

Restaurants

⭐ Alain Ducasse au Plaza Athénée   French

25 ave Montaigne   01 53 67 65 00

Curated by Ducasse with chef Christophe Moret, the
emphasis on purity and faultless preparation brings the
classical elements of haute cuisine into a contemporary

realm. The menu offers the chance to indulge to the highest magnitude, while the impeccable service and culinary perfection is guaranteed to provide memories to last a lifetime. Open for lunch Thursdays and Fridays 12:45 to 14:15 and dinner Monday to Friday 19:45 to 22:15.

Ⓜ Alma – Marceau, Map 3 F4 23

Mood
Contemporary

114 ave des Champs-Élysées
01 42 89 98 89

This swanky Franco-Asian salon is the place to meet and greet. Designer Didier Gomez has created a spicy and sexy interior with the restaurant's larger-than-life geisha photos, floating Noguchi lamps and shimmering silvery silks. And all this is a glamorous backdrop for chef Jacky Ribault's fusion menu. There is live music and DJs spinning their tunes every weekend. Mood also offers a great brunch. Open daily 10:00 to 04:00. Ⓜ George V, Map 3 E2 24

Noura
Arabic/Lebanese

27 ave Marceau
01 47 23 02 20

Head over to Noura to get your fix of high-quality gourmet Lebanese: this eatery goes way beyond the standard hummus and tabouleh. Healthy, mid-priced plates are beautifully presented and offer guests tastes of delicious regional specialities. (The wood-fired grill dishes are especially recommended). The restaurant also offers catering, and its take-away service is also a strong point. Check the website for other locations. Open Monday to Sunday 12:00 to midnight. Ⓜ George V, Map 3 E2 25

PDG

American

20 rue Ponthieu

01 42 56 19 10

Known for its great gourmet burgers, pastrami-filled bagels and live music every Thursday and Friday evening, PDG is the kind of American-esque diner where the buzzy vibe is as good as the grub. Also at 5 rue du Dragon in the 6th (01 45 48 94 40). Open Monday to Sunday 12:00 to 15:00 and 19:00 to 23:00. Ⓜ Saint-Philippe du Roule, Map 4 A2 26

Pershing Hall

International

49 rue Pierre Charron

01 58 36 58 36

The stunning decor, designed by genius Andrée Putman, is reason enough to visit Pershing Hall. This is Paris' version of the Hanging Gardens of Babylon, where a breathtaking wall covered by 250 types of foliage reaches to the clouds. It's an incomparable space for enjoying the international cuisine or imaginative cocktails. One of the city's best late night hot spots. Ⓜ George V, Map 3 E3 27

Ratn

Indian

9 rue La Trémoille

01 40 70 01 09

Rich jewel-toned colours and carved wood accents, Ratn provides an authentic taste of royal Moghul cuisine with its mid-price lunch and dinner menus; tandoori chicken, lamb saag, and homemade cheese grilled with peppers are all made with freshly ground spices and well-sourced ingredients. Restaurateur Sanjay's Delhi-born father, Chaman Lal Bhalla, is credited with popularising 'gourmet' Indian cuisine in Paris. Ⓜ Alma – Marceau, Map 3 E4 28

Le Relais de l'Entrecote

Steakhouses

15 rue Marbeuf   01 49 52 07 17

Steak frites is the only item on the menu at this mid-priced Paris institution, where melt-in-your-mouth steaks are accompanied by a sublime, secret-recipe sauce and golden *frites*. Order them *rare saignant* (rare), *bleu* (nearly rare), *à point* (medium) or *bien cuit* (well done). Reservations not accepted. Also in the 6th arrondissement (01 45 49 16 00). Dinner from 20:00. Ⓜ George V, Map 3 F4 29

Taillevent

French

15 rue Lamennais   01 44 95 15 01

Under the expert helm of chef Alain Solivérès, Taillevent's cuisine is fit for royalty: Emperor Napoleon III was a frequent 19th century dinner guest at this timelessly elegant former residence of the Duke de Morny. Stunning food and a museum-quality contemporary art collection create an extraordinary culinary experience. Open Monday to Friday for lunch at 12:15 and dinner at 19:15. Ⓜ George V, Map 3 E1 30

Bars

Le Bar du Plaza Athénée

Hôtel Plaza Athénée   01 53 67 66 00

Taking cocktailing to new heights, you will be entranced by the exquisite design contrast of sleek, ice-like bar and warm leather club chairs surrounded by gorgeous art works. Cocktails are pricey but fabulous, and the clientele appropriately chic and star-studded. Ⓜ Alma – Marceau, Map 3 F4 31

Bugsy's

8 rue de Berri   01 42 68 18 44

This animated bar advertises itself as 'the original Chicago speakeasy', replete with black and white images of gangsters and American actors on its walls. English is certainly the dominant language here, where local clientele are predominantly English, Irish and American. Knock back Guinness like water and take a break from French-speaking Paris. Ⓜ George V, Map 3 F2 **33**

Mathis Bar

3 rue de Ponthieu   01 53 76 01 62

This is yet another stylised den, its brothel-look decor invoking a debauched spirit. Hardly a new kid on the party block, the Mathis has nonetheless maintained its discreet hipster status with admirable tenacity. Notorious as a favourite cocktail hangout for the PR and film industry, the limited plush velour couches fill quickly, but they generally welcome anyone appropriately attired.

Ⓜ Franklin D Roosevelt, Map 4 B2 **32**

Nightclubs

Neo

23 rue de Ponthieu   01 42 25 57 14

Neo is like the cool table in your high school cafeteria – if your high school's cool table had booze, models, and the occasional celebrity. Small, dark, and select, nothing is particularly outstanding about this place except that it's where the beautiful people come to party, and it always delivers a good time. Ⓜ Saint-Philippe du Roule, Map 4 A2 **34**

Pink Paradise

49-51 rue de Ponthieu   01 58 36 19 20

Those seeking Paris' saucier side will love this post-club hotspot where men and women convene around the all-baring beauties: Pink is the fun and sexy late-night answer to the question 'where to next?'. Hosting one of the city's best Ladies' Nights – Pink and the City – one Friday a month, the newly opened Pink School also offers pole dancing lessons for €25. Ⓜ Saint-Philippe du Roule, Map 3 F2 **35**

Regine's

49-51 rue de Ponthieu   01 43 59 21 13

Named for the woman who established the world's first discotheque, Regine's retro-glam decor still stands strong today; think plush red seating, mirrored ceilings and walls. For a night not to be missed try Thursday's *'Au Bonheur des Dames'*. Strictly reserved for ladies, everything is free from 21:00 to 23:00, including dinner, drinks and the hottest male strippers in Paris. Ⓜ Saint-Philippe du Roule, Map 3 F2 **36**

Showcase

Under Pont Alexandre III   01 45 61 25 43

Clubs don't come much hotter than Showcase, a disco wonderland tucked under the Pont Alexandre III. Lounge around in its black leather chairs and marvel at the occasional glint of the Seine through exposed stone and metal walls. It has a reputation for being an exclusive club, though the door policy doesn't appear overtly tight. Simply come well-dressed and be prepared to wait for a bit.

Ⓜ Champs-Élysées – Clemenceau, Map 8 B1 **37**

VIP Room

76 ave de Champs-Élysées   01 56 69 16 66

Though nowadays this club generally caters to celebrities during its fashion week parties and special events, it adheres to its name with a flashy facade and glamorous bravado. Lounge on long leather couches, and check out the surrounding columns, a waterfall, and giant screens. Bathrooms – a marvel of modern design – are a force to be reckoned with following multiple cocktails.

Ⓜ George V, Map 3 F2 **38**

Gay & Lesbian

Queen

102 ave des Champs-Élysées   08 92 70 73 30

The most legendary of all gay Parisian dance clubs proves once again it is the queens who really know how to party. This behemoth is packed with scantily clad clubbers gyrating hard to the beats of the night's theme: disco Monday, house on Tuesday, Wednesday Ladies' Night, and Saturday's Metrosexual party. Entrance is €15 to €20 with one free drink. Ⓜ George V, Map 3 E2 **39**

The Islands & The Latin Quarter

This is the place for a quick world tour – it's ancient French charm on the *deux îles*, and pies, pints, and ethnic eats in the student-friendly Latin Quarter.

Fans of faux-Dublin drinking dens will find their spiritual home in the Latin Quarter, where it seems an Irish pub sits on every corner. Those that prefer a more international vibe need not fear: the vast population of local students has ensured the establishment of plenty of well-priced ethnic eating joints to meet their culinary needs.

Venue Finder

Bars	The Hideout	p.215
Bars	The Long Hop	p.215
Bars	Le Violin Dingue	p.215

Cafes

Berthillon

29-31 rue Saint Louis en l'Île   01 43 54 31 61

Parisians flock to this legendary purveyor of dreamy delights. Since 1954 three generations of the Berthillon family have created all-natural ice creams and sorbets made without preservatives or artificial flavours. Tasty offerings feature exotic choices like cinnamon, gingerbread, pear-and-caramel, and chocolate-mandarin. Encompasses both outdoor tables and a cosy the *salon de thé*. The restaurant is closed in August. Open Wednesday to Sunday 10:00 to 20:00.

Ⓜ Pont Marie, Map 13 B2 40

Ziryab

1 rue des Fossés Saint-Bernard   01 53 10 10 16

For a breathtaking view of Notre Dame and the Right Bank along the Seine, the relatively quiet rooftop terrace above the Institut du Monde Arabe offers several tables with umbrellas for those who want to enjoy afternoon tea. The building's intricately patterned and light-reactive steel shutters were designed by architect Jean Nouvel, and along with the cultural exhibits on show, makes this a must-see. Check out the viewing room adjacent to the terrace for a breathtaking panorama. Ⓜ Jussieu, Map 13 B3 41

Restaurants

Anahuacalli
Mexican

30 rue des Bernardins
01 43 26 10 20

For 10 years Cristina Prum and her warm staff have been welcoming Latin American expats and Parisians into their sunny casa to experience authentic, moderately priced Mexican cuisine. Natives swear that the nopalito (cactus) salad is as fresh as grandma's. High-quality margaritas slide down easily here. Book ahead. Ⓜ Maubert-Mutualité, Map 13 A3 **42**

L'AOC
French

14 rue des Fossés St-Bernard
01 43 54 22 52

Sophie and Jean-Philippe Lattron welcome locals and visitors in to the carnivore's paradise that is L'AOC. A former master butcher, Jean-Philippe has a discerning eye for high-quality meats and presents them well, selecting the best AOC (Appellation d'Origine Contrôlée) ingredients for his loyal clientele. Must-tries include the rotisserie, homemade terrines and *triperie* (organ meat). Ⓜ Cardinal Lemoine, Map 13 B3 **43**

Aux Anysetiers du Roy
French

61 rue Saint-Louis en l'Île
01 56 24 84 58

This intimate restaurant on Île St Louis is located in a 17th century building classified as a historic monument. Serving classic French cuisine for several decades, it has fed visitors and historical celebrities like Dali, Bardot and Jerry Lewis. Enjoy rabbit glazed with mustard on snugly-placed wooden tables and marvel at the medieval decor. Ⓜ Pont Marie, Map 13 B2 **44**

Clockwise from top left: L'AOC, Verres à vin, Dinner cruise along the Seine

Breakfast in America
17 rue des Écoles

American

01 43 54 50 28

Route 66 has been extended to Paris with this ol' fashioned diner. Craig Carlson set up shop with a boomerang-patterned counter from Philly, an iconic Cubs football helmet, and photos of movie diner scenes from Taxi Driver and When Harry Met Sally. Regulars love the Sunday brunch, bottomless cups of coffee, and non-stop breakfasts with pancakes, scrambled eggs, or bacon, and fries.

Ⓜ Cardinal Lemoine, Map 13 A3 45

El Picaflor
9 rue Lacépède

Latin American

01 43 31 06 01

This is a celebration of the international influences that have shaped Peru's healthy gastronomy, where fixed menus in all price ranges offer the chance to try specialities like fish escalope with lime and onions, or Peruvian-style lomo beef. Consult the online menu to order favourites in advance (four guests minimum). Live music on weekends creates a jovial Latin welcome. Ⓜ Jussieu, Map 15 D1 46

Foyer du Vietnam
80 rue Monge

Vietnamese

01 45 35 32 54

This tiny, low-key joint packs a peppery punch. Several styles of savoury phos, bô-kho, and bô-bun with nems are a few examples of the authentic cuisine on offer. Try the crab sauteed to order, or artisanal Vietnamese ice cream quê huong in cinnamon, fig, coconut and ginger flavours. Students receive a discount. Ⓜ Place Monge, Map 15 D1 47

Le Jardin des Pâtes
4 rue Lacépède

Vegetarian
01 43 31 50 71

Since 1984 these affable gardeners have been 'growing' the freshest, tastiest pasta in town; all grains used in the homemade pasta are organic. Wheat, rice, barley, rye, buckwheat, and chestnut pastas are made fresh onsite and creatively cooked. Try the rice pasta with sauteed vegetables, ginger and tofu. Meat options are also available, along with organic beers and juices. Ⓜ Jussieu, Map 15 E1 49

La Mosquée
9 rue Saint-Hilaire

Moroccan
01 43 31 38 20

Vibrant mosaics and murals, gingerbread wood details and pointed arches provide eye candy in this open, airy wonder. Aromatic north African tagines tempt the taste buds, while the hammam, *gommage*, and massage treatments soothe the soul. Try the *formule*-with-a-twist, an opportunity to indulge all the senses. Ⓜ Place Monge, Map 15 E2 50

Sabraj
175 rue Saint-Jacques

Indian
01 43 26 70 03

Every bit of this 14th century dining room has been meticulously decorated with the vibrant colours, rich woods and silky textures of Mumbai, creating a romantic ambience to taste traditional specialities cooked in the earthen tandoor. The wide assortment of naan breads, biryanis and curries in varying degrees of spiciness are recommended. Open everyday 12:00 to 14:30; 19:00 to 23:30.
Ⓜ Cluny – La Sorbonne, Map 12 E4 48

Bars

The Bombardier

2 pl du Panthéon   01 43 54 79 22

This is perhaps the most English pub in Paris, where little,
if any, attempt at speaking French is made by the staff. No
wonder so many English feel right at home here. Take in the
view of the Panthéon from the terrace or join the students for
the Sunday night quiz. Ⓜ Cardinal Lemoine, Map 12 F4 **51**

Le Caveau des Oubliettes

52 rue Galande   08 26 10 12 87

One of the greats of the city's live music scene, des Oubliettes
is a drinking den from the Middle Ages: descend the
precarious stone staircase into two adjoining caves; one for
the bar and one for the performances. Des Oubliettes features
varied musical genres, including indie, folk, and incredible
jazz and blues jam sessions. Ⓜ Cluny – La Sorbonne, Map 12 F2 **52**

Connolly's Corner

12 rue de Mirbel   01 43 31 94 22

The colourful and eye-catching artwork covering the outside
of this bar gives an alternative edge at odds with images of a
typical Irish pub. Step inside, however, and the atmosphere
is pure Paddy. The area's students keep Connolly's happily
in business, and the place jumps during darts tournaments.
Live music sessions take place on Tuesday, Thursday, and
Sunday. Ⓜ Censier Daubenton, Map 15 D2 **53**

The Hideout

11 rue du Pot de Fer   01 45 35 13 17

Fun and vibey, The Hideout has some of the lowest drink prices in Paris. Its widespread popularity spawned a second location across the river in the 1st at Châtelet (46 rue des Lombards, 01 40 28 04 05), boasting the same super happy hours lasting from 16:00 to 21:00. There are seven huge screens for sports fans. The first location remains a longstanding student bar for mixed internationals.

Ⓜ Place Monge, Map 15 C2 54

The Long Hop

25-27 rue Frederic Sauton   01 43 29 40 54

Large and spacious with a big outdoor terrace, this English pub with an American feel hosts a wide range of cultures and generations: you find a broad mix of activities from live DJs, to a round of billiards or darts. Tuesday is Ladies' Night and weekends turn the pub in to a pick-up haunt.

Ⓜ Maubert-Mutualité, Map 12 F2 55

Le Violin Dingue

46 rue de la Montagne St-Geneviève

'The Mad Violin' is an appropriate translation for this late night bar – it's renowned for orchestrating a bit of madness. Just behind the looming Panthéon, it is a favourite stop-off point when the rest of the bars have shut. Reminiscent of an American fraternity party, this is probably the closest thing you'll come to a typical college bar in Paris.

Ⓜ Cardinal Lemoine, Map 12 F3 56

Going Out

Louvre, Tuileries & Opéra

One part Karl Lagerfeld, one part Mona Lisa, these *quartiers* are a mix of fashionable eateries and over-priced tourist traps.

Chic and well-established are the by-words for the fashionable eateries which huddle between the Louvre and the Opéra; places such as Hôtel Costes, Angelina's and Davé will never fall out of favour. That's not to say that every restaurant is on the best-dressed list; Au Pied du Cochon is an example of a restaurant well-worn but well-loved. A warning, however, that eating and drinking in such a high-profile tourist zone can prove expensive.

Venue Finder

Cafes

Angelina

226 rue de Rivoli   01 42 60 82 00

Angelina is a slice of Parisian folklore, serving what many claim to be the city's best hot chocolate; tourists flock here for steaming pitchers of melted African dark chocolate served alongside a silver bowl brimming with frothy Chantilly cream. Polished marble and sparkling mirrors create an elegant ambience in this 1903 landmark, once favoured by Coco Chanel and Marcel Proust. Ⓜ Concorde, Map 4 F4 **57**

Brasserie Printemps

66 blvd Haussmann   01 42 82 58 84

Magic awaits you under the awe-inspiring stained-glass dome created in 1923 for the department store Printemps

Haussmann. The interior was redesigned by Didier Gomez with art deco motifs and modern lines. Centred around the dome is a seafood bar serving oysters and lobster. On a par with the glittering ambience is the seasonal French cuisine by top-notch chef Alain Cirelli. Many appreciate the high-quality yet moderately-priced, brasserie fare with a twist. The veal piccata, and roasted sea bass are favourites, as is the afternoon tea accompanied by handmade sweets. Occasionally wine tastings are hosted by noted producers of the Pays d'Oc; just give them a call to sign-up. Open Monday to Saturday 09:00 to 19:00 (Thursday evenings until 22:00).

Ⓜ Havre-Caumartin, Map 4 F1 58

Le Café Corrazza 1787

12bis rue de Montpensier,
11-12 Galerie Montpensier　　　　　01 42 60 13 52

Named after its 1787 founder, Signor Corrazza, this location has hosted upscale guests within the park-like courtyard of the Palais Royal for over 200 years. (General Napoléon Bonaparte was reputed to be an ice cream aficionado who frequented for the famous maraschino cherry variety.) Today dine on mid-priced Italian fare like antipasti and bruschetta, alongside a range of couscous dishes.

Ⓜ Palais Royal Musée du Louvre, Map 9 C1 59

Café Marly

93 rue de Rivoli Cour Napoléon　　　　01 49 26 06 60

In the Richelieu wing of the Louvre, this Costes brothers' enterprise continues to be a see-and-be-seen spot in the

Clockwise from top left: Hamaika, Le Café Corrazza 1787, Brasserie Printemps

LE CAFÉ CORRAZZA 178

Parisian cafe world. Fashion designers and press check each other out over a coffee and upper-end bistro fare in the stately crimson and gold space. High style and dress are *de rigueur*. Ⓜ Palais Royal Musée du Louvre, Map 9 C2 60

Restaurants

Au Pied du Cochon   French
6 rue Coquillière   01 40 13 77 00

If you've ever wondered where to satisfy that early morning craving for oysters or French onion soup, look no further. Just next to St Eustache church, this institution in Les Halles has been serving tourists and locals all day everyday for over 60 years. If you are really craving something extraordinary order heaped seafood platters of grilled pigs' feet with béarnaise sauce (the brasserie's namesake dish).

Ⓜ Les Halles, Map 9 E1 61

Au Trappiste   Belgian
4 rue Saint Denis   01 42 33 08 50

This jeans-and-kid-friendly Belgian brasserie offers a lively chance to experience divine *moules frites*, where generous mussel portions are steamed in various aromatic sauces and broths. The beer selection is predominantly Belgian and the lodge-like decor conjures up a trappist monastery through warm, honeyed wood tones and faux stained glass windows. Other menu options include grilled sausages with sauerkraut or *crêpes*. Ⓜ Châtelet, Map 9 F3 62

Cuisine & Confidences
33 pl du Marché St Honoré

Contemporary
01 42 96 31 34

Healthy and tantalising creations pepper the menu at Cuisine & Confidence, a sprawling restaurant in this hip courtyard. Go for cumin-marinated tuna with shrimp, or an apple and foie gras crumble. Brunch on Saturday and Sunday is a family affair, with a plentiful sweet and savoury spread. The red blankets for terrace tables are a nice touch.

Ⓜ Tuileries, Map 5 A3 63

Davé
12 rue de Richelieu

Chinese
01 42 61 49 48

Paris' hottest fashion designers, models and entertainment moguls vie for the best tables at this Chinese and Vietnamese restaurant: most loyalists never consult a menu, simply letting Davé take care of them. Regulars have included Karl Lagerfeld, Leonardo DiCaprio, Gwyneth Paltrow, and Stella McCartney. Reservations are based on fashion clout and the menu is pricey. Ⓜ Palais Royal Musée du Louvre, Map 9 B1 64

Hamaika
11 rue Jean-Jacques Rousseau

Spanish
01 40 28 91 15

Walking into Hamaika is like entering a rustic mountain cabin; the cosy dining room is lined with wide planks of reclaimed wood displaying framed art, photos, books and knickknacks, while the Basque-style tapas menu (on blackboard) spans an entire wall. Well-portioned, mid-priced tasty titbits such as Serrano ham, fish soup, and crème catalane are enjoyed in a relaxed, lively atmosphere. Ⓜ Louvre Rivoli, Map 9 D2 65

Mori Venice Bar
Italian

2 rue du Quatre Septembre   01 44 55 51 55

Philippe Starck's vision of bringing to Paris the 'pure Venetian' cuisine he savours at his homes in Burano has come alive through a partnership with the ever-gracious Massimo Mori of the famed Emporio Armani Café. Food is authentic and the space infuses classic Venetian glamour with a Starck-esque sensibility. Order the linguini and keep an eye out for Zidane.

Ⓜ Bourse, Map 5 C3 66

Le Saut du Loup
International

107 rue de Rivoli   01 42 25 49 55

Finally, a museum restaurant that doesn't serve stale, prehistoric relics better suited to the archives. Enter chef Pascal Bernier's foie gras accented with anise, or scallops with a cinnamon *soufflé*. This is a refined yet comfortable setting offering spectacular views from its first-floor dining room.

Ⓜ Tuileries, Map 9 B1 67

Le Soufflé
French

36 rue du Mont Thabor   01 42 60 27 19

Little fluffy clouds of flavour await diners at Le Soufflé, a cosy space specialising in, obviously, *le soufflé*. The emmental and *comté* cheese is a perennial favourite, so too the wild mushroom. The fixed-price menu is reasonably priced, especially if including the Grand Marnier dessert *soufflé* – the bottle is left on the table to consume as desired.

Ⓜ Concorde, Map 4 F4 68

Victoria Station

La Victoire Suprême du Cœur
41 rue des Bourdonnais

Vegetarian
01 40 41 93 95

Traditionally Parisian fine dining has offered few options for non-meat eaters, so vegetarian and vegan diners – and their carnivorous friends – will be overjoyed to discover the inspired, healthy menu at La Victoire Suprême du Cœur. Savour roasted mushrooms with blackberries, handmade pasta or green tea icecream with hazelnut cream, all created with fresh, non GM ingredients. Alcohol is not served.

Ⓜ Châtelet, Map 9 E2 69

Victoria Station
11 blvd Montmartre

Contemporary
01 42 36 73 90

Forget the Eurostar; this restaurant offers instant transportation not just to London, but back though time to

the early 20th century. The interior is outfitted with authentic dining cars acquired from London's Victoria Station in the 1940s, the restaurant's decor has ruby velvet banquettes, fringed lampshades and brass luggage racks that add to the adventurous spirit. Ask to sit in the second dining room for a more complete immersion into the locomotive theme. This is a fun, casual spot for families and groups of friends to enjoy the well-priced menu featuring wood-fired pizzas and grilled meats. The pizza *au chèvre* with goat's cheese, ham and *crème fraîche* is a customer favourite. They don't take reservations, so be prepared for the occasional short queue.

Ⓜ Grands Boulevards, Map 5 D2 **70**

Bars

Barlotti Lounge
35 place du Marché St Honoré   01 44 86 97 97

Upstairs from a stylish Italian restaurant, this fabulous little cocktail bar boasts fantastic bellinis, including exotic choices expanding on the traditional recipe. Decor is cosy and intimate, with dark wood panelling, big couches, and candles on every table, plus low-key music and impeccable service. Right in the heart of the city, it's open every night of the week until 02:00. Ⓜ Pyramides, Map 5 A3 **71**

Harry's Bar
5 rue Daunou   01 42 61 71 14

An old favourite, Harry's Bar has a reputation that precedes itself. Birthplace of the bloody mary, dedicated drinkers pay homage at this temple of inebriant ingenuity. Dark wood panelling and memorabilia traces back to its 1911 opening, offering a laid back environment. The downstairs piano bar offers live music Tuesday to Saturday from 22:00. Try the famous hot dogs. Ⓜ Opéra, Map 5 A3 **72**

Hemingway Bar Hôtel Ritz
15 place Vendôme   01 43 16 30 31
One of the best bars with one of the best bartenders, this is an essential stop in your tour of literary and luxurious Paris. The old-fashioned bar and library panelled walls create a warm setting for the fancy patrons to mingle and imbibe. Though pricey, you get your money's worth with impeccable service and fantastic drinks. Ⓜ Tuileries, Map 5 A4 **73**

Hôtel Costes
239 rue St Honoré   08 26 10 12 86
The Costes is the unequalled Parisian haunt for trendy lounge lizards and the jet-set. A glance around the room will confirm time has not diminished its panache; the luxury and grandeur of the interior with its rich velvets, reds, wood and seductive lighting are quintessential Paris. The DJ is sound perfect and the terrace is lovely in summer Ⓜ Tuileries, Map 4 F4 **74**

Kitty O'Shea's
10 rue des Capucines   01 42 96 02 99
After a long day battling the fashionistas in the boutiques of rue St Honoré, sometimes you just want to have a drink where someone's going to know your name – welcome

to Kitty O'Shea's. This bar is a sporting hub that draws the crowds for the annual Six Nations rugby tournaments. There's also trivia night of a Wednesday, and a traditional Irish band plays every Sunday. Ⓜ Opéra, Map 5 A3 **75**

Kong

1 rue du Pont Neuf   01 40 39 09 00

Most famous to visitors as the setting of Carrie's awkward lunch with the ex in Sex and the City, Kong offers breathtaking views alongside sushi and cocktails on the top floor of the Kenzo building. The futuristic kitsch decor is vintage Philippe Starck. Very small, it fills up fast. Things get clubby late on weekends. Ⓜ Pont Neuf, Map 9 D3 **76**

Willi's Wine Bar

13 rue des Petits Champs   01 42 61 05 09

The legendary Willi is one of the founding fathers of the Paris wine bar scene. And as terminally un-chic as the name may be, this 1930s style bar is legend. One of the first to introduce the idea of integrating the wine bar with a full menu restaurant, Willi's offers numerous wines by the glass. This is a favoured haunt for Anglophones. Ⓜ Bourse, Map 5 C4 **77**

Nightclubs

Le Cabaret Club

2 pl du Palais Royal   01 58 62 56 25

It's clear to see why 'Le Cab' once seduced Paris' social elite. Even the looming presence of the Louvre near the entrance cannot detract from the luxurious and stylish interior, with sensual coloured lighting, and plush, secluded alcove seating. Its heyday may have passed but, it still remains a popular spot for tourists. The cover price varies, but is generally €20 and includes a drink ticket. Entry is free with dinner in the restaurant. Ⓜ Palais Royal Musée du Louvre, Map 5 C1 **78**

Le Paris Paris

5 ave de l'Opéra   01 42 60 77 02

Put a gritty basement dive behind velvet ropes with discerning doormen, throw in some great music and you suddenly have a hotspot. Despite the rather grimy ambience of this former gentleman's club, Le Paris Paris has become an über-sceney locale for the fashion, art and music crowds. More punk than chic, the music alternates between electro DJs, europunk and rock. Get there early if you want to make the cut. Ⓜ Pyramides, Map 9 B1 **79**

Gay & Lesbian

La Champmesle

4 rue Chabanais   01 42 96 85 20

This lesbian bar benefits from its placement just a few blocks from the beautiful Opéra Garnier. The dim lighting, wood, and exposed stone make this a great place to meet for a fun and lively evening. Thursday and Saturday evenings welcome singers and live performers, and Tuesday brings fortune-telling with a psychic. Local art exhibitions are also on show each month. Ⓜ Pyramides, Map 5 C3 **80**

Montmartre & Pigalle

Kitsch is the word in this *quartier*, where restaurants double as galleries and edgy bars and restaurants capitalise on Pigalle's sexy past.

Pile on the bohemian threads and brush up on your knowledge of contemporary art: these two areas bring an interesting vibe to the mix that is Paris. The cobble stone 'village' of Montmartre is known as a magnet for the young and arty, while Pigalle calls to a youthful and energetic crowd keen to imbibe the buzz emanating from the quarter's transformation from sex-dive to saucy hotspot.

Venue Finder

Cafes

Café des Deux Moulins

15 rue Lepic   01 42 54 90 50

Once the film set where Audrey Tatou portrayed the good-hearted waitress Amélie Poulain, this now famous cafe in Montmartre has since become a must-do for nostalgic fans. Fortunately there're still some locals with a newspaper at the copper-topped bar, and the movie-themed touches don't overwhelm the authentic 1950s design. The cafe is open 07:00 to 02:00 every day. Ⓜ Blanche, Map 2 B2 🔟

No Stress Café

2 place Gustave Toudouze   01 48 78 00 27

Chill out and soak up the positive energy – and satisfying food – at this favoured hang-out of the neighbourhood's artistically-inclined. Enjoy a pre-show cheeseburger or post-performance cocktail. The brightly coloured wall murals and mismatched cushions set the tone for the Thursday to Saturday evening tarot card readings and massage therapy. Sunday brunch overlooking the courtyard is lovely.

Ⓜ Saint-Georges, Map 2 C4 🔢

Restaurants

Le Basilic   French

33 rue Lepic   01 46 06 78 43

Journey through the winding cobblestone streets of Montmartre to discover this intimate, ivy-covered nook dating back to 1830. A former inn, the original hand-carved walnut bar, bookcases and expansive stone fireplace have been retained to create a perfect setting to enjoy a well-priced traditional French meal in a non-smoking environment. Perfect for a romantic candlelit date or a relaxed lunch. Ⓜ Blanche, Map 2 B2 83

Hôtel Amour
8 rue de Navarin

Contemporary
01 48 78 31 80

This is a see-and-be-seen spot for Paris' denizens of cool. A new addition to Thierry Costes' repertoire, Hôtel Amour is a quirkily designed by-the-hour hotel (in homage to the racy reputation of its Pigalle neighbourhood.) The courtyard garden gushes with greenery, and the simple cuisine is surprisingly well-priced. Delicious Sunday brunch is packed with bed-headed bohos. Open daily 12:00 to 23:30.

Ⓜ Saint-Georges, Map 2 C4 84

Living B'Art
15 rue la Vieuville

Contemporary
01 42 52 85 34

Well-priced, honest food with a side of philosophy is Living B'Art's offering. The venue promotes evenings of cultural exchange through art exhibits, spellbinding gypsy jazz, literary discussions, and theatrical presentations, alongside creative meals made with fair-trade or equitable commerce ingredients. Eat *charcuterie* plates, vegetable-stuffed tarts, hearty soups and unique garden salads at long, communal tables. Book ahead, as this small *atelier* fills quickly every night. Closed Monday and Tuesday. Ⓜ Abbesses, Map 2 C2 85

Rose Bakery

46 rue des Martyrs

British

01 42 82 12 80

Always friendly, Rose Carrarini and husband Jean-Charles create daily menus with dishes like kedgeree (a British recipe with rice and fish), bangers and mash, and English cheeses with homemade chutney. Get in early for delectable baked goods – scones, shortbread, and carrot cake usually sell out by 14:30. Open for lunch and weekend brunch, come for the best muesli in Paris. Ⓜ Saint-Georges, Map 2 D4 86

Spring

28 rue de la Tour d'Auvergne

Contemporary

01 45 96 05 72

An overnight sensation, Chicago chef Daniel Rose is shaking up the establishment (and winning them over) handling everything from reservation to food shopping; Rose still manages the time to create deliciously imaginative cuisine. Moderately-priced and with only 16 tables, booking is essential. Open for dinner Tuesday to Friday; lunch also on Thursday and Friday. Ⓜ Cadet, Map 2 D4 87

Wally Le Saharien

36 rue Rodier

Moroccan

01 42 85 51 90

Monsieur Wally's friendly souk-like restaurant offers a mystical evening of culinary adventure. A mix of textiles, delicately carved chairs, and tribal artefacts provide the perfect setting to experience the signature 'dry' couscous with slow-cooked lamb and zesty merguez sausage. On Saturday evenings listen to darbouka hand drums and romantic naï flutes. Fixed price dinners (€39). Ⓜ Saint-Georges, Map 2 D4 88

Bars

Corcoran's

110 blvd de Clichy   01 42 23 00 30

In one of Pigalle's saucier districts, Corcoran's has become a favoured post-performance watering hole for the lovely Moulin Rouge dancers. It's a lively, convivial hangout where expats convene for a pint, a meal, or to watch one of the regular live bands. Corcoran's St Michel locale (28 rue St André des Arts, 01 40 46 97 46) is equally festive.

Ⓜ Blanche, Map 2 A2 87

The Ice Kube

1-5 psg Ruelle   01 42 05 20 00

Kube Hotel's new concept bar is not for feeble-bodied boozers: half an hour is all you are allowed in the retro pop hotel's glacial bar, where you don giant parkas, mittens and optional boots to protect against the -5°C temperature. For €38 indulge in 30 minutes of all you can drink, deliciously flavoured Grey Goose vodkas. Ⓜ La Chapelle, Map 1 D1

O'Sullivans

92 blvd de Clichy   01 42 52 24 94

O'Sullivans By The Mill, next to the famous Moulin Rouge, feels and looks more like a club than the Irish pub it claims to be, with vast open spaces and a back room dedicated entirely to the DJ. Staff are friendly and outgoing, and the crowd is always ready for fun. Open 'til dawn, this is a favourite late-night stop. Ⓜ Blanche, Map 2 A2 90

St-Germain des Prés & Odéon

Tick off another tourist must-do, and drink in history in the shadow of literary greats at any one of St-Germain's numerous Belle Epoque cafes.

Home to Café de Flore, Les Deux Magots and Le Procope (ancient eateries all three) St Germain is heavy on the cafe culture. Pull up a seat, linger over an espresso and watch the world pass by. The area also maintains a few upscale establishments which – along with the haute boutiques – continue to draw the fashion crowd to the Left Bank.

Venue Finder

Café de Flore

Cafes

Café de Flore

172 blvd St-Germain   01 45 48 55 26

Famed rival of Les Deux Magots, Café de Flore has hosted
many greats; Trotsky, Sartre, Signoret, Hemingway, Capote,
Bardot, Dali, Bacall, De Niro… not to mention the stars and
French intellectuals of today. Serving a menu of omelettes,
salads, and club sandwiches, it's the perfect spot to people

watch. Theatrical readings and philosophy debates keep the cafe's creative history alive. Ⓜ St-Germain-des-Prés, Map 12 B1 ⁹¹

Les Deux Magots

6 place St-Germain des Prés   01 45 48 55 25

Intellectuals of the Left Bank have debated politics, philosophy, and literary merit for around 100 years at this legendary institution; Gide, Malraux and Hemingway have all been regulars. Today it still attracts a philosophical local crowd, albeit mixed with a good deal of casually-dressed tourists. In truth, the beauty of this scandalously priced cafe lies in soaking up the history. Ⓜ St-Germain-des-Prés, Map 12 B1 ⁹²

Restaurants

Brasserie Lipp   French

151 blvd St-Germain   01 45 48 53 91

Along with neighbours Les Deux Magots and Café de Flore, Brasserie Lipp completes the St-Germain des Prés 'holy trinity' from the Belle Époque era. This celebrated establishment is one of Paris' original upscale Alsatian-style brasseries, intertwined with visionary figures since it beginnings in 1880. It features regional sausages, and pork with sauerkraut along with a huge beer selection. Ⓜ St-Germain-des-Prés, Map 12 B1 ⁹³

Fish La Boissonerie   Seafood

69 rue de Seine   01 43 54 34 69

This former *poissonnerie* (fish shop) now serves a wide range of fresh seafood. Colourful mosaic tiles and fun fish sculptures create a friendly, low-key vibe. With co-owners from New Zealand and the US, a mid-priced menu and an extensive wine list, Fish has become a popular destination for English-speaking expats. Ⓜ Mabillon, Map 12 C1 94

Huîtrerie Régis
3 rue de Montfaucon

Seafood

01 44 41 10 07

The twinkling-eyed Régis welcomes his guests as friends into this 14-seat cabana. The magical oysters are sourced from Marennes Oléron in partnership with culturist Claude Garnier, owner of restaurant Huîtrerie Garnier in the 16th (117 avenue Mozart, 01 40 50 17 27). Pair them with Daniel Crochet's flinty sancerre. Shrimp or a scallop terrine are on the menu for non-oyster addicts. Ⓜ Mabillon, Map 12 C1 95

Le Procope
13 rue de l'Ancienne Comédie

French

01 40 46 79 00

Le Procope is reputed to be the oldest cafe and restaurant in Paris, having opened its doors in 1686. The world's first encyclopaedia was written here, and Benjamin Franklin even polished up the American constitution over a coffee or two. Today it draws tourists, literati and intellectuals who gather around spectacular shellfish platters. A living museum.
Ⓜ Odéon, Map 12 C2 96

Ze Kitchen Galerie
4 rue des Grands Augustins

International

01 44 32 00 32

High ceilings and snow white-walls hung with rotating exhibits of vivid art, create a modern air in William Ledeuil's hotspot, just a few doors down from Picasso's old studio. The simple decor is an elegant backdrop for his inspired palette of flavours assembled from his Asian travels. Named 2006 Chef of the Year by Gault Millaut, reservations are a must.

Ⓜ Saint-Michel, Map 12 D1 97

Bars

Alcazar Mezzanine Bar

62 rue Mazarine   01 53 10 19 99

With a modern, minimalist feel, the DJ bar upstairs from Terrence Conran's Alcazar restaurant is the epitome of a chic Parisian lounge. The light, open space attracts a contingent of well-dressed professionals and pretty-young-things, making it a favourite amongst the international crowd. The stylish decor combined with the laid-back atmosphere and snacks available upstairs make it the ideal cocktail venue.

Ⓜ Odéon, Map 9 C4 98

Au Père Louis

38 rue Monsieur Le Prince   01 43 26 54 14

A truly authentic Left Bank experience, Au Père Louis offers a traditional Toulousain restaurant next door to its immensely popular wine bar. With its exposed stone walls and original beams, the bar attracts a predominantly local clientele. Large old wine barrels serve as tables to perch your wine upon. If there is enough space, pull up a wooden stool and settle in. Ⓜ Odéon, Map 12 D3 99

Le Bar du Marché

75 rue de Seine   01 43 26 55 15

A mainstay in vibey cafe culture, 'Le Marché' remains a great place to get a drink with a fun crowd. On warm nights be ready to wait (or fight) for a table outside –the prime pavement seating looking over the lively pedestrian street of rue du Bucci. Ⓜ Mabillon, Map 12 C1 **100**

Coolin

15 rue Clément   01 44 07 00 92

With its ideal setting snugly tucked beneath the beautiful arches of the Marché St-Germain, the vast wooden warmth of the Coolin welcomes all who pass through its doors. The terrace is a picture perfect spot to enjoy a beer and a burger, while evenings take a livelier turn with happy hour from 17:00 to 20:00. There is live music at 17:00 Sundays.

Ⓜ Mabillon, Map 12 C2 **101**

L'Echelle de Jacob

10-12 rue Jacob   01 46 34 00 29

This is a homely place to drink with friends. That being, of course, if your home resembles an über-stylish meeting place of the terminally hip. One of the *quartier's* few upscale cocktail bars, L'Echelle's small location fills up quickly with local trendies drinking some of Paris' best martinis. A tall staircase, presumably Jacob's ladder for which the bar is named, leads to a second level that has tables accommodating bigger groups. Ⓜ Mabillon, Map 12 B1 **102**

The Frog & Princess

9 rue Princesse   01 40 51 77 38

The Princess brings the best of English pub life to the Left Bank. Long tables set the scene for socialising and make this a great place to let loose with a fun-loving convivial crowd. Tuesday is student night. Also check The Frog and Rosbif (116 rue St Denis, 2nd, 01 42 36 34 73). Ⓜ Mabillon, Map 12 B2 **103**

The Mazet

61 rue St Andre des Arts   01 43 25 57 50

A favourite stop The Doors' fans, The Mazet is allegedly the site of Jim Morrison's last hurrah. Officially an English pub with a vast English-speaking staff and clientele, it nonetheless maintains a Euro feel. Live bands offer great entertainment, and a DJ spins Friday and Saturday until 05:00. Reasonably priced drinks sweeten the appeal. Ⓜ Odéon, Map 12 C1 **104**

La Palette

43 rue de Seine   01 43 26 68 15

La Palette is a safe haven where the decor, menu, and crotchety old waiters remain stubbornly in place. Yet despite the ambiguity of its appeal, the simple cafe with its little round tables remains an old-favourite: youthful hipsters head here when the sun shines. Ⓜ Mabillon, Map 12 C1 **105**

Pub St-Germain

17 rue de l'Ancienne Comédie   01 56 81 13 13

This 'pub' is in fact a stylish three-storey cocktail establishment with a late night restaurant. The decor is refined and majestic with comfortable couches, interesting chairs, and romantic lighting achieved by various lamps and candles. Music highlights the ambience, and the wonderful selection of drinks makes this a great place to drink with friends. Happy hour is 18:00 to 20:00. Ⓜ Odéon, Map 12 C1 **106**

Le Théâtre

2-4 rue du Sabot   01 45 48 86 47

This newcomer has the potential to draw some of the social sleek back to the somewhat abandoned Left Bank. Relatively large by Parisian standards, a theatrical mezzanine puts it somewhere between club and cocktail bar. But where cosiness is lost, sexiness and intimacy are gained by its red tones, candles, velvet motif walls and a mirror on the ceiling. The dramatic are invited to flaunt their moves on stage to a repertoire of classics. Ⓜ St-Germain-des-Prés, Map 12 A2 **107**

Nightclubs

Castel

15 rue Princesse   01 40 51 52 80

Castel is one of the few truly private 'members only' clubs in Paris, bringing a bit of much-needed panache to St-Germain's nocturnal happenings. An elite enclave, members have access to private areas of the three-storey mansion while visitors can dine, drink or dance in the basement club. PS – you don't need to be a member to enter, simply dress like one. Ⓜ Mabillon, Map 12 B2 **108**

Trocadéro & Les Invalides

Cool clubs and elegant restaurants – many with killer views – mingle with the *quartier's* grand monuments and stunning museums.

It makes sense that the area boasting some of the city's most recognisable landmarks also hosts some of the city's most dramatic restaurants and bars. If you're looking for that picture-postcard view or want to mix with Paris' movers and shakers, you'll find venues here in which to see and be seen. From the newly revamped Jules Verne at the top of the Eiffel Tower to the stunning Cristal Room Baccarat, this is old-money Paris at its bourgeois best.

Venue Finder

Café d'Esplanade

Cafes

Café d'Esplanade
52 rue Fabert   01 47 05 38 80

Situated across from Les Invalides, Café d'Esplanade is
another striking alliance of the Costes brothers' backing
and Jacques Garcia's design flair. Favoured by politicians,
government officials and journalists, this swanky, late-night
bistro also offers an airy terrace during summer. Order the
club sandwich with bacon or smoked salmon, a signature
favourite on the upwardly-priced menu. Open every day
08:00 to 01:30. Ⓜ La Tour Maubourg, Map 8 A3 **109**

Restaurants

L'Arbre de Sel
138 rue de Vaugirard

Korean
01 47 83 29 52

Crispy seafood *galettes*, bibimbap with vibrant vegetables and exotic lotus flower roots, and an invigorating homemade kimchi relish are just a few of the tasty and colourful delights to be discovered in this most welcoming Korean restaurant near Montparnasse. Fresh decor is enhanced by local art exhibits, the owners are charming and the well-priced, generous dishes have the locals raving. Ⓜ Falguière, Map 1 C4

Bateaux Parisiens
pte de la Bourdonnais

Dinner Cruises
01 46 99 43 13

Watching Paris slip by while drifting down the Seine is romantic; but paired with exceptional cuisine it is unforgettable. Indulge with chef Yves Gras' all-inclusive, high-end menus before dancing to live music. Smart-casual dress and reservations essential. Lunch cruises 12:45 to 14:30; dinner cruises 20:30 to 23:00. Ⓜ Bir-Hakeim, Map 7 C2 **111**

Benkay
Novotel Tour Eiffel, 61 quai de Grenelle

Japanese
01 40 58 21 26

The rooftop restaurant in the Novotel exhibits a spectacular panorama of the Seine, Maison de la Radio, and Paris' Statue of Liberty, where you will eat artful sushi as well as shabu shabu (hot pot) and teppanyaki on the tableside iron griddles. Many claim this upscale haven offers the best authentic, gourmet Japanese cuisine in town. Ⓜ Bir-Hakeim, Map 1-B3

Cristal Room Baccarat

Cristal Room Baccarat
11 pl des États-Unis

Contemporary
01 40 22 11 10

Gliding down the red carpet embedded with countless glittering lights, visitors to the Philippe Starck-designed Baccarat showroom feel as glamorous as the crystal on display. The restaurant turns the drama up a notch further, where chef Thierry Burlot draws upon his Bretagne heritage to create upscale dishes based on regional ingredients. Popular with the city's beautiful people. Ⓜ Iéna, Map 3 C3 **110**

Jules Verne
The Eiffel Tower

French
01 45 55 61 44

A new chapter was written into the history of the Jules Verne restaurant in 2007, as under the helm of Alain Ducasse the

'modern classic' French cuisine has risen to even greater heights. Pricey options include a six-course tasting menu in the evenings or a lunch *formule*. Minimum two-month advance bookings required. Ⓜ Bir-Hakeim, Map 7 C3 112

Kambodgia
Vietnamese

15 rue de Bassano
01 47 23 31 80

The dramatic interior of this south-east Asian gem combines intimate teahouse with opulent opium den. The food is similarly stunning. Enjoy mainly Vietnamese and Cambodian fare like ginger fish wrapped in banana leaves, caramelised pork with coconut sauce, or the many styles of dim sum and barbecue. The green tea macarons are superb. Ⓜ Iéna, Map 3 D3 114

Les Ombres
International

27 quai Branly
01 47 53 68 00

This addition to the Parisian landscape is on the rooftop of the Musée du Quai Branly, offering a view of the Eiffel Tower. Chef Arno Busquet celebrates world cultures with his use of intriguing and often fair-trade ingredients into classical cuisine. Perfect for a special occasion. Dinner reservations essential. Ⓜ Alma – Marceau, Map 7 D2 113

Bars

Concorde Atlantique

Porte de Solférino opp 8 quai Anatole France   01 47 05 71 03

The wonders of the Seine have finally been capitalised upon, where Paris' champagne-swilling youth can put their sea legs to the test without taking one of the cliched cruises. Docked just off the place de la Concorde, this rocking little terrace is the summer's answer to a Riviera escape for those willing to choose murky green over crystal azure. Live DJs and funky tunes ensure it's always packed.

Ⓜ Assemblée Nationale, Map 8 D2 115

Nightclubs

Aqua
5 ave Albert de Mun   01 40 69 23 90

CinéAqua is a unique concept that offers a stunning aquarium, concerts, a cinema, Japanese restaurant Ozu, and by night a pulsating nightclub called Aqua – all in one unbelievable location. The originality of the entire complex extends to the club itself, whose stylish interior and fashionable crowd dance beside the enormous and majestic aquarium. Ⓜ Iéna, Map 7 B1 116

Black Calvados
40 ave Pierre de Serbie   01 47 20 77 77

Some of the biggest names in the nightlife business (including Chris Cornell of Soundgarden fame) pulled together to reinvent the legendary Calvados of the '60s and '70s. The inspired result is Black Calvados. Clientele, including celebrities and the city's party elite, can eat pseudo-American cuisine upstairs before descending to rock out surrounded by smoked mirrors, stainless steel and glowing cube tables.

Ⓜ George V, Map 3 E3 117

Entertainment

The grand cabarets aren't the only option for a night of cultural entertainment; Paris' streets are filled with spectacles of all kinds.

Cabaret & Strip Shows

Cabaret exists today as the quintessential Parisian experience for visitors. It appears in two forms; that of the cabaret-dinner-and-drinks variety, and the more artistic expression of the French *chanson*, which will be lost on those who do not know any French. The former is highly sought after, with shows possessing a Las Vegas-style quality thanks to their grand costumes and classy choreography. Dancers are often topless but the spectacle maintains its Parisian class.

Au Lapin Agile

22 rue des Saules   01 46 06 85 87

An institution, Au Lapin Agile has been drawing locals and curious visitors to get a glimpse of its old Montmartre venue for about 150 years. Less glamorous than other venues, there is no dinner option, just a charmingly ancient and dimly lit room where performers entertain with a variety of musical and comedy acts (you may enjoy the content more if you speak French.) You can come and go as you please between 21:00 and 02:00. Entry is €24, which includes one drink. Additional drinks €7. Ⓜ Lamarck – Caulaincourt, Map 1 D1

Crazy Horse

12 ave George V   01 47 23 32 32

As the name implies, performances here are a slightly raucous mix of magic, comedy, and skilful stripteases. The theatre is small and intimate, offering dinner packages with nearby participating restaurants pre or post show. Seating is first come, first serve. Arrive early. Ⓜ George V, Map 3 E3 **118**

Le Paradis Latin

28 rue Cardinal Lemoine   01 43 25 28 28

This little gem set away from pack on the Left Bank has a very lively show with acrobatics, wonderful lighting effects, and great choreography. A very Parisian cabaret. Dinner and a show costs from €117 to €170; champagne and a show is €82.
Ⓜ Cardinal Lemoine, Map 13 A4 **119**

Lido

116bis ave desChamps-Élysées   01 40 76 56 10

Lido is still one of the most extravagant shows in Paris. Home to the famous Bluebell girls, it has all the glitz and glam of a Las Vegas act. Prices for dinner and the show start at €140, or opt for the show only, with a half-bottle of champagne for €90 to €100. There's a matinee option on Tuesday and Sunday costing from €80 to €125. Ⓜ George V, Map 3 E1 **120**

Michou

80 rue des Martyrs   01 46 06 16 04

Treat yourself to an unforgettable alternative cabaret experience at Michou. Frequented mostly by locals, French-speakers will better appreciate the nuances and humour. Though the entertainment value of this eccentric and fun drag show will certainly not diminish regardless of what's lost in translation. Dinner and show €99 (book in advance).

Ⓜ Abbesses, Map 2 D3 **121**

Moulin Rouge

18 blvd de Clichy   01 53 09 82 82

Since its debut in 1889, the Moulin Rouge has remained the most famous cabaret venue in the world, made only more so by the Hollywood film and its trademark red windmill. But be warned; the influx of tourism can detract from the authentic sex appeal, turning the venue into an amusement park attraction. Dinner and show €145 to €175 (depending on menu choice); show only €99 (includes a half-bottle of champagne). Ⓜ Pigalle, Map 2 C3 **122**

Casinos

Though they may lack the glitz and glamour that draw the masses to the true gamblers paradise of Las Vegas, Paris' eight casinos are certainly stylish. Perhaps the most popular establishment with travellers, due to its location on the Champs-Élysées, is the Aviation Club de France which offers a wide range of games and services.

Cinemas

Paris has a great passion for film which allows for a wide range of traditional and original cinematic entertainment. A few pointers: For non-French films, be sure they are being

Moulin Rouge

played in VO (*version originale*), the original language with French subtitles. VF films (*version francais*) are dubbed into French without subtitles. Tickets can be anywhere from €5 to €10. Count on only the larger cinemas, like the UGCs and the Gaumont, to offer basic food concessions. Serious film aficionados should check out the Cinémathèque Française, a film museum, library, and research centre in a Frank Gehry-designed dwelling that also sponsors daily screenings. Summer is the time for open-air festivals, with one at Parc de la Villette in July and August. In mid-August, the Cinéma au Claire de la Lune event sees films screened in parks and public squares around the city. Check listings in the weekly Pariscope, on sale at newsstands. Or check online at www.allocine.com, where reservation of tickets online is possible.

Comedy

French comedy can be difficult to appreciate as a foreigner, even with a solid grasp of the language. Still, if your French is outstanding you may appreciate some of the more local venues like L'Ane Rouge in the 17th (3 rue Laugier, 01 43 80 79 97) or La Grande Comédie in the 9th (40 rue de Clichy, 01 48 74 03 65). Indulge your Anglo-centric sense of humour with the production company, Laughing and Music Matters. It regularly hosts some of the best English speaking stand up comedians from around the world at venues throughout Paris. Check out www.anythingmatters.com for details.

Live Music

Live music is a vibrant part of the Paris nightlife scene. Summer brings with it numerous festivals; look out for Solidays for AIDS awareness on the first weekend in July (www.solidays.org); techno at the Techno Parade on the third Saturday in September (www.technopol.net); the two-day Rock-en-Seine festival at the end of August (www.rockenseine.com); and world music throughout the summer for Quartier d'Eté (www.quartierdete.com). On June 21st every year the Fête de la Musique has musicians playing on every street corner all night long. Also popular is the Paris Jazz Festival in May. Look to Pariscope for acts and concerts, available at *kiosques*.

Opera

Opera appreciation runs high in Paris, due largely to the fact that the city boasts two of the most magnificent opera houses; the classic and luxurious Palais Garnier and the ultra modern Opéra Bastille. Occasional performances are also run in the Théâtre des Champs-Élysées or the Théâtre du Châtelet.

Those that can't afford premier tickets can try for same-day, reduced price tickets at one of two theatre *kiosques* at place de la Madeleine in the 8th, or Esplanade de la Tour Montparnasse in the 14th (visit www.kiosquetheatre.com for available tickets – in French). Last minute tickets are sometimes available at the box office half an hour before the showing for as little as €6 or €7, but visibility is usually very limited. Get there at least an hour before and be prepared to queue.

Theatre

The French flair for the dramatic has led to the proliferation of theatrical venues throughout Paris. From small and intimate to lavish and impressive, you can be entertained in the setting of your desire pretty much any night of the week. Ticket prices range anywhere from €10 to close to €100, depending on the establishment and popularity of the production. Reduced prices are available for students. Or buy same-day tickets at a 50% reduction.

Many of the theatre performances are in French, though certain venues (Théâtre de Nesle, Odéon Théâtre, and Sudden Théâtre), will usually have at least one production in English each season. Find performance listings in Pariscope, available at *kiosques* which you will usually find around the metro station exits. Check www.parisvoice.com for listings in English.

Profile

Culture

A giant canvas of museums, theatres, concert halls and sculpture, Paris is a living, breathing monument to the artists of the past and the future.

Rich Cultural Heritage

Paris' history is intertwined with its love of art and its ties to the Catholic church. In the middle ages, Paris grew in prominence as a result of its status as a place of religious worship, welcoming Catholics to its magnificent Notre Dame Cathedral and the Sainte Chapelle. It became a magnet for students at the same time, growing rapidly into the European seat of higher education. Continuing through the centuries, Paris has been an inspiration to its residents and its visitors.

Museums like the Louvre and the Musée d'Orsay house priceless works of art, and lesser known galleries throughout the city nurture burgeoning talents. The Panthéon serves as the final resting place for French greats, while the Académie Française ensures the language of those greats is protected. Classic Haussmann-style apartment buildings stand across the street from new-wave glass-facade structures, denoting a city at once rich in history yet moving forward.

People

This Parisian dichotomy between tradition and modernity is as evident in its varying architecture as it is in the clash of social classes that has rocked the city and the nation in recent years.

Immigrant waves began arriving from former colonies in the 1950s, adding a new spice to Parisian life. France was not ready for such changes, and integration has been difficult for many.

The *banlieue* riots of October and November 2005 stemmed from the accidental deaths of two boys from the eastern suburb of Clichy-sous-Bois. After weeks of unrest throughout the country, order was restored, but tension remains high. The 2007 election of right-wing 'law and order' President Nicolas Sarkozy only served to remind many non-European French citizens and immigrants that their culture remains at odds with some of the traditions of France.

Religion

The once dominant Roman Catholic faith has seen its numbers diminished considerably in France over the last 30 years. Though the government does not compile statistics on religion, most independent polls reveal that the French majority no longer actively practise any faith, with an increasing percentage giving over to atheist or agnostic beliefs. The number of 'culturally Catholic' French is somewhere around 85%, though regular churchgoers make up a tiny constituency. But through all this, Catholic churches still dominate the landscape of Paris. This is not to say, however, that other religions fail to get a look-in: Protestant churches are represented in smaller numbers; a community of several hundred thousand Jews resides in Paris, predominantly in the Marais quarter; while the 5th *arrondissement* is home to La Mosquée de Paris (built after the second world war, it is the central place of worship for an increasing Muslim population).

A secular French government guarantees freedom of worship, though in 1995 Parliament created a Commission on Cult Activities, reporting a list of cults that it considers potentially dangerous, including the Church of Scientology and Jehovah's Witnesses. Despite its secular claims, half of France's national holidays are Catholic feast days. No other faith's holy days are officially recognised by the state.

Food & Drink

French in origin, the common usage of the word 'cuisine' indicates just how important French cooking is to the rest of the world. The French tradition of *haute cuisine*, literally 'high cuisine,' dates back to the mid 16th century, when Catherine de Medici arrived from Italy to marry the future French King Henri II. Importing her own team of chefs, she combined their skill, and the French crown's wealth, to nurture cuisine as an art form. Later, Louis XIV's Versailles feasts were known for their many courses, the first instance where food was not served all at once. Down through the years, famous French chefs such as La Varenne, Carême, Escoffier and Bocuse have codified, refined, and developed French cuisine into what it is today. Receiving a makeover in the 1960s, modern French now combines the tradition of laboriously prepared sauces with lighter *nouvelle cuisine,* developed from the kitchens of Paul Bocuse and others.

But while advancements will be made, France will always remain a country whose food is defined by its regions; foie gras and speciality duck dishes from the south-west; creamy sauces from Normandy; south-east spice; *choux croute* from the north-east, to name but a few. Wine remains an essential part of any fine meal, as does a plate of seasonal assorted cheeses. The different eating establishments include *cafés*, which often serve sandwiches and light meals (mostly over lunchtime hours), *bistros* serving dishes such as *steak frites* and regional dishes as mentioned above, and *brasseries*. The latter have their roots in the Alsace region but again serve similar fare to *bistros*. Both *bistros* and *brasseries* serve quality food for reasonable prices in the evening.

However, the city is no longer a place strictly dedicated to indigenous cuisine. Immigrants from North Africa have brought with them their own specialities, and Chinatown in the 13th *arrondissement* offers a variety of good Chinese restaurants. Several Irish, English and international bars and various American burger joints also dot the capital.

For groceries, there are markets (see p.164) selling fresh cheese, fruit and meat, and large supermarket chains include Monoprix and Champion. Smaller grocery stores, known as *épiceries*, stay open until midnight and can be found on street corners in most areas. Larger *hypermarchés* such as Carrefour and Leclerc skirt the city.

Time To Eat

Parisian restaurants operate around strict hours, so keep this in mind when planning your day. Lunch is served from midday until 14:30, while the evening sessions start at 19:00 until 22:00 during the week and 23:30 at the weekend.

History

Saintly saviours, headless queens, marauding invaders and modern governments; Paris has remained strong over thousands of years of change.

Lutèce

Originally named Lutèce, Paris was a thriving city in Roman Gaul. As the Roman Empire declined, Attila the Hun's marauding forces encroached upon France from the east. The prayers of Saint Geneviève were answered when Attila's army surprisingly turned south before entering the city. Saint Geneviève remains the patron saint of Paris, her statue standing guard over the Pont de la Tournelle.

Capital Of Kings

In 508AD, Clovis I, the first king of the Franks, established his capital in Paris. Though Charlemagne moved the French capital to Aachen, Paris reassumed its status as capital city thanks to Hugues Capet.

Over the course of the 12th century, many churches sprang up across the city, notably on the Left Bank. In 1163, construction began on the Cathedral of Notre Dame on Île de la Cité, the larger of Paris' two islands. The Left Bank developed as a centre of learning, and as Latin was the language of scholars, the area became known as the Latin Quarter. Meanwhile on the Right Bank, the focus was on finance and commerce and building began on the Louvre Palace.

Assemblée Nationale

A History Of Violence

While kings, scholars and clergy lived well in the capital, the poor and merchant classes began to crumble under intolerable living conditions. Charles V quashed a 1358 rebellion, and built the infamous Bastille fortress to defend against insurrections. Great political instability and religious intolerance culminated in the St Bartholomew's Day Massacre in 1572, when nearly 3,000 Protestants were killed by Catholic mobs. A Protestant king, Henri IV ascended to the throne only after he converted to Catholicism in 1594, uttering his famous line, 'Paris is well worth a mass'. Henri IV

proved worthy of Paris as well, creating the Place des Vosges and the Louvre's Cour Carrée. Paris continued to bloom in the 17th century, which saw construction of the magnificent Palais du Luxembourg, the Palais Royal, and the rebuilt Sorbonne. Political unrest persisted in the city, however, and Louis XIV moved the court to Versailles, 20 kilometres west of the city.

Revolution & Terror

The French nobility lived lavishly at Versailles, while people starved in the capital's streets during the 18th century. However, on July 14, 1789, an angry Paris mob ransacked the arsenal and freed a handful of political prisoners at the Bastille, sparking the French Revolution. The following years saw the city descend into a bloody 'Reign of Terror', where a guillotine was erected at the current-day Place de la Concorde. There, in 1793, Louis XVI and his queen, Marie Antoinette, were both beheaded.

19th Century

Order was finally restored to the city by the young army officer, Napoleon Bonaparte. Later crowning himself Emperor, Napoleon I expanded the French Empire through military conquests. He transported Egyptian obelisks to the city and built the Roman-style church of La Madeleine.

Paris received a mid-century makeover, thanks to Emperor Napoleon III's prefect Baron Haussmann. Demolishing many neighbourhoods, Haussmann made way for the wide boulevards for which Paris is known today. Napoleon III also commissioned a monument to his uncle's military victories, the Arc de Triomphe, at the head of the Champs-Élysées. In 1889, the Eiffel Tower was constructed as a temporary structure during the World Exhibition held in Paris. The tower, an iron and steel symbol of modern architecture, proved useful as a radio antenna and endures as the symbol of Paris.

War

Though Paris never became a battleground during the first world war, French casualties were painfully high, and the city suffered through periods of rationing and flu epidemic. Between wars, Paris was the alluring, exotic city that drew literary giants and jazz luminaries to its cafes and clubs. However, the arrival of the Depression plunged city and nation into disarray, transforming France in to an easy target for the vengeful German forces who occupied Paris in June 1940. The government evacuated Paris and took up residency in Vichy, where it became a puppet of the Nazi regime. Nazi rule lasted four years, marked by the forced deportation of Paris' Jewish residents from their homes along the rue des Rosiers in the Marais district. Their destination was Auschwitz. Yet it was also a period of heroism, as the French Resistance movement fought clandestinely against their oppressors. As Allied forces advanced toward Paris in the summer of 1944, Resistance movements within the city stepped up, skirmishing with German commander Von Choltitz's troops.

General Leclerc's French army division arrived to find Von Choltitz in retreat, thus sparing the city any major damage.

End Of The Empire

As post-war France's empire crumbled, immigrant influxes from former colonies saw a need for inexpensive housing. Unattractive *banlieues* were created outside of Paris, where great poverty and strong racial divisions exist to this day. Charles De Gaulle, second world war hero, came out of retirement to assume the reigns in 1958 as first president of the Fifth Republic. De Gaulle quit the presidency 10 years later, his popularity waning partly due to the Algerian War and the series of student riots in May 1968.

Modern Marks

Fifth Republic presidents have followed in the footsteps of kings before them, putting their own stamps on the city with varying degrees of success. While the bizarre tube and glass facade of the Centre Pompidou and the Pyramid at the Louvre have become interesting novelties, other modern constructions such as the Opéra Bastille and the universally detested Tour Montparnasse are often met with revulsion. Jacques Chirac left office in May 2007 after 12 years as president, a period marked by scandal, *banlieue* rioting, economic stagnation and political promises left unfulfilled. New President Nicolas Sarkozy, son of immigrants and champion of a smaller government, hopes to reinvigorate the economy by relaxing taxes on businesses, among other initiatives.

Clockwise from top left: Le Panthéon, Mémorial de la Déportation, Palais Royal

Paris Timeline

250BC	Celtic Parisii tribe establishes fishing village on banks of the Seine.
52BC	Julius Caesar seizes control of Gaul, quashing revolt led by Vercingetorix.
250AD	St Denis, Paris' first bishop is martyred at Montmartre.
506	Clovis I makes Paris capital of his Merovingian dynasty.
987	Hugues Capet establishes Capetian Dynasty, which will last in France until the Revolution.
1100	Famous monk Abelard begins teaching in Paris.
1150	Population reaches 50,000.
1163	Construction begins on Notre Dame.
1257	Sorbonne (University of Paris) opens.
1320	Population reaches 250,000.
1328	England's Edward III claims French throne; Hundred Years' War begins.
1572	St Bartholomew's Day Massacre.
1789	Storming of the Bastille (July 14). The French Revolution ensues.

1792	September 22 – 'Day 1 of Year 1 of the French Republic' proclaimed.
1804	Napoleon crowns himself emperor.
1870-1871	Prussian army sieges Paris for four months; citizens eat zoo animals.
1889	Moulin Rouge cabaret opens.
1900	Paris metro makes its first trip.
1914	'Miracle of the Marne': 600 Parisian taxis help transport reserve infantry to early battle during the first world war.
1924	Paris hosts Summer Olympic Games.
1940	German army occupies Paris.
1944	Paris liberated (August).
1958	The Fifth Republic under De Gaulle.
1968	Huge student protests in Latin Quarter.
1995	Jacques Chirac elected President.
1997	Jospin's socialist government is elected.
2001	Bertrand Delanoë elected mayor.
2003	Heatwave kills thousands.
2005	Riots erupt in the suburbs.
2007	Nicolas Sarkozy elected President.

Paris Today

Finding the balance between romance and commerce, history and development, bustle and Zen, Paris today looks towards a vibrant future.

Paris is one of the most popular tourist destinations in the world. In 2006, it welcomed some 27 million visitors. Part dreamy monument, part hard-edged cosmopolitan city, the City of Paris has been working hard to ensure her two parts integrate harmoniously: the swathe of new bike paths, the Velib' city bicycle programme, new bus and taxi-only lanes, laws requiring the clean-up of doggie doo, and hordes of little green municipal trucks doing daily street cleaning all work together to ensure Paris remains a functioning, modern city. At the same time, construction of the business district of La Défence, just outside the reach of inner city Paris, has ensured the city preserves its village vibe with restaurants, boutiques and well-preserved Haussmanian apartment buildings.

The face of Paris is also in constant transformation. With the opening of EU borders, the population is a mix of born-and-bred French, among people of African, Eastern European and Asian descent; each ethnic group introducing new traditions, languages and foods to ensure an enriched city landscape. The English language, as the official business language of Europe, is becoming more widely understood, although a sprinkling of French goes a long way to currying favour and garnering good feeling. And as the people

View over the Seine

change, so does the backdrop. Ever since Baron Haussmann carved out wide boulevards and spurred citywide rebuilding efforts in the latter half of the 19th century, Paris has undergone frequent facelifts. Currently, the eastern and north-eastern parts of the city are seeing the majority of the new construction. While real estate is always at a premium, aesthetics and ecology remain of utmost importance, as architects and city planners strive to create functioning, environmentally sound works of art in which Parisians can live, work and play. The 12th *arrondissement* has recently seen completion on the Ateliers de Paris building, a complex of workshops dedicated to new development in fashion and design. Located on rue de Faubourg St Antoine, the space brings together artists and designers in a new way, connecting them with major industry drivers. And there are many more new developments to follow.

New Projects

Bibliothèque Médiathèque Bagnolet

Spring 2009 brings with it the opening of this modern, five storey public library. With over 4,000 sq m of space, it will be largely dedicated to a DVD and CD collection and will feature a meeting room to accommodate 100 people.

Carreau des Halles

The Forum des Halles will be demolished to make way for an innovative combination of green space and shopping in central Paris, due for completion in 2012. La Canopée, a futuristic glass ceiling, will cover much of the grounds. Along with retail space, a 3,000 sq m conservatory and a '21st century cafe' will overlook 4.3 hectares of park space. Eco-friendly, the park's glass canopy will contain solar cells, and its unique structure will allow for rain-gathering to form a reservoir with which the gardens can be watered.

Grand Projet de Renouvellement Urbain

The Grand Projet de Renouvellement Urbain (GPRU) was begun in 2001 with the longterm objective of improving the quality of life in 11 main neighbourhoods across the city. Many projects are planned or are underway in the 18th and 19th *arrondissements*, including the improvement of public squares, as well as the construction or renovation of low-cost housing. The 12th and 20th are currently undergoing improvement to traffic flow problems on avenue de la Porte de Vincennes, rue Noël Ballay and rue Fernand Fourreau.

Le 104

This 19th century building at 104 rue d'Aubervilliers in the 19th is set to open its doors in late 2008, welcoming contemporary artists and their fans. The 35,000 sq m property will hold up to 5,000 people. As part of a larger urban renewal project for north-east Paris, 'Le 104' will feature a large main hallway, from which visitors will find artwork in all its stages, from conceptualisation to exhibition. In the meantime, head to 11bis rue Curial to see what's going on. Visit www.104.fr for more.

Paris Biopark

Located in the 13th *arrondissement*, Paris Biopark is developing into a centre for public health companies and biotechnology firms. With 700,000 sq m of office space and another 450,000 sq m of activity space, the facility can house up to 60,000 personnel. Along with numerous small biotech firms, various companies in other sectors already taking up residence there include the Accor Group, Les Caisses d'Epargne and La Caisse des Dépôts. Visit www.parisdeveloppement.com for more information.

La Philharmonie de Paris

A joint venture between the City of Paris and the national government, the new auditorium at Parc de la Villette in the 20th will hold 2,400 spectators for orchestra performances. The Paris orchestra will make its home here, while the venue will also host musical acts from around the world. The 20,000 sq m space will also feature many private rehearsal rooms. It is due to open in November 2012. Visit www.philharmoniedeparis.com.

Maps

Map 1

Paris Overview

N

LA GARENNE-COLOMBES
ASNIÈRES-S-SEINE
SAINT-OUEN
Porte de St-ouen
CLICHY
Porte de Clichy
BOULEVARD BESSIÈRES
COURBEVOIE
LEVALLOIS-PERRET
BATIGNOLLES
18t
BOULEVARD PÉRIPHÉRIQUE
AVENUE DE CLICHY
La Grande Arche
Porte d'Asnières
Porte de Champerret
17th
2
MON
PIGA
9
L'ARCHE
LA DÉFENSE
PUTEAUX
A14
NEUILLY-SUR-SEINE
BOULEVARD BINEAU
AVE DU ROULE
Porte Maillot
CHARLES DE GAULLE
Place de Mal Juin
AVE DE VILLIERS
Place du Gal Catroux
MONCEAU
BOULEVARD DES BATIGNOLLES
Gare St-Lazare
ST LAZARE
AVE DES TERNES
Place de la Porte Maillot
Porte Dauphine
3
Arc de Triomphe
ÉTOILE
Champs-Elysées
4
8th
5
OPERA
GI
BOU
BOIS DE BOULOGNE
Porte de la Muette
Place du Trocadéro
Place de la Concorde
1st
Porte de Passy
7
TROCADÉRO
Eiffel Tower
CHAMP DE MARS
8
LES INVALIDES
Jardin des Tuileries
Hôtel des Invalides
9
Musé du Lou
ST GERMAIN DES PRÉS
ODÉ 6th
16th
PASSY
ALLÉE DES FORTIFICATIONS
11
7th
12
BOULEVARD RASPAIL
A13
Porte d'Auteuil
Place de la Pte d'Auteuil
BOULEVARD DE VERSAILLES
BEAUGRENELLE
RUE DE LA CONVENTION
15th
14
Tour Montparnasse
MONTPARNASSE
EXELMANS
Porte de St-Cloud
Place de la Pte St Cloud
Gare Montparnasse
Place Denfert Rochereau
POI
BOULOGNE-BILLANCOURT
Quai d'Issy
Porte de Sèvres
BOULEVARD VICTOR HUGO
RUE D'ALÉSIA
14th
ÎLE ST-GERMAIN
Porte de la Plaine
Porte de Brancion
Porte de Vanves
Porte de Châtillon
Porte d'Orléans
MEUDON
ISSY-LES-MOULINEAUX
VANVES
MALAKOFF
MONTROUGE

© Explorer Group Ltd. 2008

A   B   C

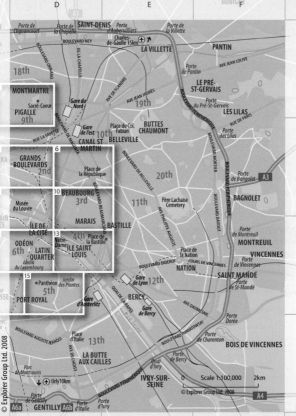

Map 1

Paris Overview

© Explorer Group Ltd. 2008

© Explorer Group Ltd. 2008

Scale 1:100,000

0   2km

275

Legend

These maps detail the most interesting areas of Paris for visitors. Restaurants, bars, shops, museums and places to explore are marked with colour-coded symbols (see below) that correspond to the numbered symbols accompanying the reviews and write-ups throughout the guide.

There's a large pull-out map at the back of the book, giving an overview of the city and highlighting the main areas of interest. Inside the back cover you'll also find a map of Paris' Metro system, and on the facing page there's an index of the city's main roads, with a grid reference allowing you to find that road on the maps.

🔟 **Essentials** 🔟 **Exploring** 🔟 **Sports & Spas** 🔟 **Shopping** 🔟 **Going Out**

Legend

🄷 *Hotel*	Built Up Area/Building	Highway
🏛 *Heritage/Museum*	Industrial Area	Major Road
➕ *Hospital*	Stadium	Secondary Road
Park/Garden	7th Arrondissement	Other Road
Pedestrian Area	★ Visitor Attraction	*Porte des Lilas* Junction Name
Shopping	⛪ Church	⌇⌇⌇ Tunnel
Education	Petrol Station	▥▥▥ Steps
Land	✉ Post Office	—Ⓡ--- *RER*
Cemetery	**MARAIS** Area Name	—Ⓜ--- *Metro*
		—◰--- *Railway Station*

Maps

277

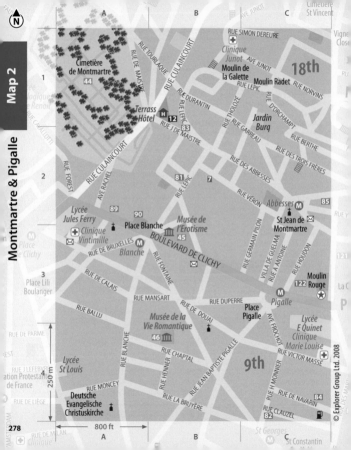

Map 2

Montmartre & Pigalle

278

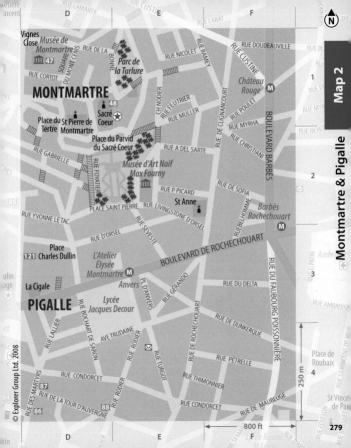

Map 2

RUE LAMARCK

RUE CUSTINE

RUE LABAT

incent

RUE DOUDEAUVILLE

D

E

F

Vignes
Close

Musée de
Montmartre

47

RUE DE LA
BONNIE

RUE CORTOT

SQUARE
DU MONT CENIS

RUE NICOLET

RUE RAMEY

RUE CUSTINE

Parc de
la Turlure

Château
Rouge

MONTMARTRE

CH NODIER

RUE FEUTRIER

RUE MULLER

RUE DE CLIGNANCOURT

RUE POULET

RUE MYRHA

BOULEVARD BARBÈS

48

Sacré
Coeur

RUE RICH

Place du
Tertre

St Pierre de
Montmartre

RUE CHRISTIANI

RUE MYRH

Place du Parvid
du Sacré Coeur

RUE A DEL SARTE

1

RUE GABRIELLE

Musée d'Art Naif
Max Fourny

RUE DE SOFIA

RUE FOYATIER

RUE P PICARD

St Anne

Barbès
Rochechouart

2

RUE YVONNE LE TAC

PLACE SAINT PIERRE

RUE LIVINGSTONE D'ORSEL

RUE DE ROCHECHOUART

M

RUE D'ORSEL

RUE SEVESTE

Place
Charles Dullin

121

L'Atelier
Elysée
Montmartre

BOULEVARD DE ROCHECHOUART

M

La Cigale

Anvers

PL D'ANVERS

RUE GÉRANDO

RUE DU DELTA

RUE DU FAUBOURG POISSONNIÈRE

Ambro

3

PIGALLE

Lycée
Jacques Decour

RUE LALLIER

RUE BOCHART DE SARON

AVE TRUDAINE

RUE RODIER

RUE TURGOT

RUE DE DUNKERQUE

RUE AMBROISE

RUE DES MARTYRS

RUE CONDORCET

RUE RODIER

RUE PÉTRELLE

Place de
Roubaix

4

87

RUE DE LA TOUR D'AUVERGNE

88

RUE CONDORCET

RUE THIMONNIER

RUE DE MAUBEUGE

St Vince
de Pa

86

250 m

800 ft

D

E

F

279

© Explorer Group Ltd. 2008

Map 3

	A	B	C

RUE P et C MORANO

RUE DE TILSIT

R RUE DE TILSIT

RUE LE SUEUR

RUE DE SAÏGON

RUE RUDE

Charles de Gaulle Étoile

M de Charles de Gaulle Étoile

★ L'Arc de Triomphe

Place Charles de Gaulle

AVE FOCH

AVE FOCH

AVE FOCH

ÉTOILE

AVE VICTOR HUGO

RUE DE PRESBOURG

AVE D'IÉNA

Musée Dapper

RUE LÉONARDO DE VINCI

RUE LEROUX

Clinique Victor Hugo

RUE PAUL VALÉRY

RUE GEORGES VILLE

RUE LAURISTON

Kleber **M**

AVE DES PORTUGAIS

Centre de Conférences Internationales

St Georges 🏛

RUE LA PÉROUSE

RUE DUMONT D'URVILLE

RUE A VACQUERIE

Place de l'Uruguay

RUE GALILÉE

RUE RAYMOND POINCARE

Victor Hugo M

Fbg St Honoré

Place Victor Hugo

Centre de Reservoirs de Passy

RUE COPERNIC

Hôtel Victor Hugo ✉

RUE BOISSIÈRE

Ste Thérèse

RUE LAURISTON

RUE CIMAROSA

AVE KLEBER

RUE DE BELLOY

16th

Marché St Didier

AVE RAYMOND POINCARE

RUE LAURISTON

RUE LÉO DELIBES

M Boissière

RUE BOISSIÈRE

RUE DE L'AMIRAL HAMELIN

1 10
52

Musée Baccarat 🏛

Square Thomas Jefferson

Place Amiral de Grasse

Lycée Assomption

Place Rochambeau ✉

RUE DE LÜBECK

RUE SAINT DIDIER

Musée Guimet 🏛 **57**

Iéna M

Place de Tokyo

RUE DE LO...

7

Place d'Iéna

PONT... WILSON

250 m

800 ft

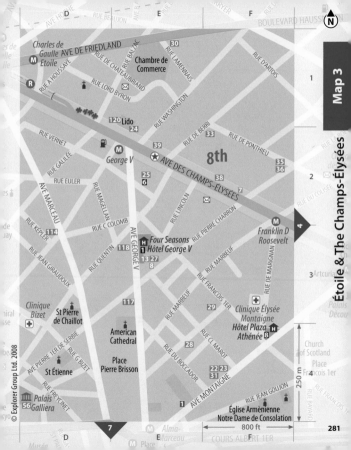

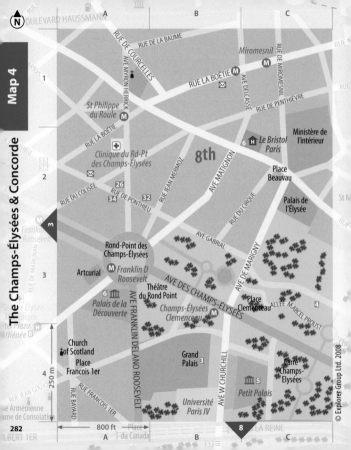

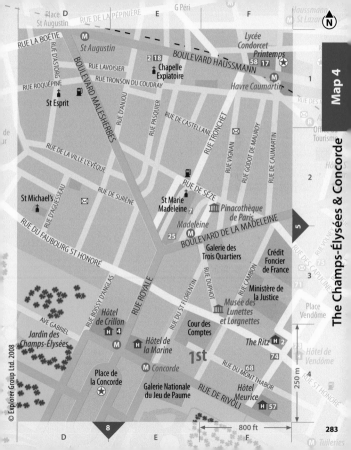

Map 4

The Champs-Élysées & Concorde

Place D
St Augustin

RUE DE LA PÉPINIÈRE

G Péri

Haussmann
St Lazare

Lycée
Condorcet
Printemps
58 17

RUE LA BOÉTIE

St Augustin

BOULEVARD HAUSSMANN

RUE D'ASTORG

RUE LAVOISIER

2 18
Chapelle
Expiatoire

Havre Caumartin

RUE ROQUÉPINE

RUE TRONSON DU COUDRAY

RUE DE CASTELLANE

RUE DES

St Esprit

BOULEVARD MALESHERBES

RUE D'ANJOU

RUE PASQUIER

RUE TRONCHET

RUE VIGNON

RUE GODOT DE MAUROY

RUE DE CAUMARTIN

Office
Tourism

RUE DE LA VILLE L'EVÊQUE

de
r

St Michael's

RUE DE SURÈNE

RUE DE SÈZE

2

RUE D'AGUESSEAU

St Marie
Madeleine 7

Pinacothèque
de Paris

RUE DU FAUBOURG ST HONORÉ

Madeleine
25

BOULEVARD DE LA MADELEINE

5

RUE DES CAPUCINES

Galerie des
Trois Quartiers

Crédit
Foncier
de France

3

71

RUE BOISSY D'ANGLAS

RUE ROYALE

RUE DU FLORENTIN

RUE DUPHOT

RUE CAMBON

Ministère de
la Justice

Place
Vendôme

Musée des
Lunettes
et Lorgnettes

AVE GABRIEL

Jardin des
Champs-Élysées

Hôtel
de Crillon
4

Cour des
Comptes

1st

The Ritz 2

Hôtel de
Vendôme

H

74

M

Hôtel
de la Marine

RUE DU MONT THABOR

68

4

RUE ST HONORÉ

Place de
la Concorde

Concorde

Hôtel
Meurice

250 m

Galerie Nationale
du Jeu de Paume

RUE DE RIVOLI

57

© Explorer Group Ltd. 2008

8

D

E

F

800 ft

Tuileries

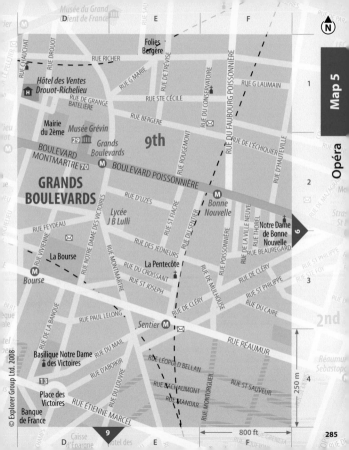

Map 6

Canal St-Martin

N

St Laurent

RUE DES RÉCOLLETS

Jardin
Villi

RUE DE PARADIS

RUE A

B

RUE ST

C

LEC
Charles de
Gaulle

RUE MARTEL

Mosque

BOULEVARD DE MAGENTA

1

Château d'Eau

BOULEVARD DE STRASBOURG

BOULEVARD DE MAGENTA

RUE DU FAUBOURG ST MARTIN

RUE DE NANCY

COUR DES PE TITES ÉCURIES

Mosque

RUE D'ENGHIEN

RUE G GOUBLIER

RUE DE METZ

Marché
St Martin

Jacques
Bonsergent

2

RUE DE MAZAGRAN

Mosque

RUE BOUCHARDON

RUE DU CHÂTEAU D'EAU

Strasbourg
St Denis

CITÉ RIVERIN

RUE TAYLOR

RUE DE LANCRY

5

Musée de
l'Éventail

RUE RENÉ BOULANGER

BOULEVARD
ST DENIS

RUE ST PHILIPPE

RUE STE APOLLINE

3

RUE STE FOY

RUE BLONDEL

BOULEVARD ST MARTIN

RUE MES LAY

RUE DE TRACY

RUE ST MARTIN

RUE NOTRE DAME DE NAZARETH

Caveau de la
République

2nd

3rd

Réaumur
Sebastopol

Musée
des Arts et Métiers

39

RUE VAUCANSON

RUE MONTGOLFIER

RUE VOLTA

RUE DU VERTBOIS

Lycée
Turgot

RUE DE TURBIGO

4 m

250 m

Musée
National des
Techniques

RUE DES FONTAINES
DU TEMPLE

RUE DE TEMPLE

St Nicolas des
Champs

Arts et
Métiers

RUE REAUMUR

© Explorer Group Ltd. 2008

10

A

B

C

800 ft

Square au

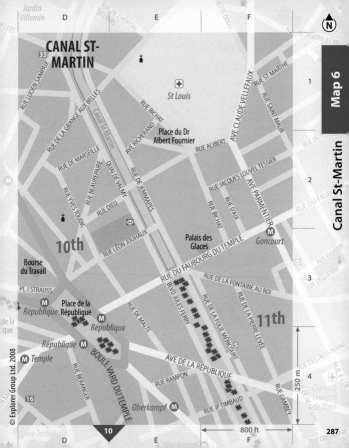

Map 6

Canal St-Martin

CANAL ST-MARTIN

33

RUE LUCIEN SAMPAIX

RUE DE LA GRANGE AUX BELLES

RUE DE MARSEILLE

RUE YVES TOUDIC

RUE BEAUREPAIRE

RUE DIEU

QUAI DE VALMY

Canal St-Martin

RUE DE JEMMAPES

RUE BICHAT

RUE RICHERAND

St Louis

Place du Dr Albert Fournier

RUE ALIBERT

AVE CLAUDE VELLEFAUX

RUE ST MARTHE

RUE SAINT MAUR

RUE DU FAUB

RUE JACQUES LOUVEL TESSIER

RUE BICHAT

RUE D'AIX

AVE PARMENTIER

10th

RUE LÉON JOUHAUX

Palais des Glaces

RUE DU FAUBOURG DU TEMPLE

Goncourt

Bourse du Travail

PL J STRAUSS

République

Place de la République

RUE DE MALTE

RUE DE LA FONTAINE AU ROI

BLVD JULES FERRY

RUE DE LA FOLIE MÉRICOURT

RUE DE LA PIERRE LEVÉE

11th

République

République

Temple

RUE BÉRANGER

BOULEVARD DU TEMPLE

AVE DE LA RÉPUBLIQUE

RUE RAMPON

RUE JP TIMBAUD

RUE GAMBEY

Oberkampf

Clinique Léonard de Vinci

250 m

800 ft

16

Lycée Technique

10

Map 7

Musée Guimet

Place
de Tokyo

3

RUE DE LONGCHAMP   Place d'Iéna

A   B   C

AVE DU PRÉSIDENT WILSON

RUE DE MAGDEBOURG

TROCADÉRO

116 Gonseil
Économique
et Social

16th

M Trocadéro

AVE D'ALBERT DE MUN

RUE FRESNEL

Place du Trocadéro
et du 11 Novembre

Musée de
l'Homme
Chaillot

Port de la
Bourdonnais

1

Place
José Marti

Palais de
Chaillot

AVE G V DE SUÈDE

AVE DE NEW YORK

Musée
de la Marine

AVE A TER DE MONACO

2

Jardin
Trocadéro

Place de
Varsovie

111   QUAI BRANLY

École St Louis
de Gonzague

RUE LE NÔTRE

PONT D'IÉNA

RUE HARDIN

AVE DU PRÉSIDENT KENNEDY

La Seine

★

112
Eiffel Tower
49

3

AVE GUSTAVE EIFFEL

Champ de Mars
Tour Eiffel

R

Parc du
Champ de Mars

4

AVE RENÉ BOYLESVE

PONT DE BIR HAKEIM

Stade Emile
Anthoine

AVE DE SUFFREN

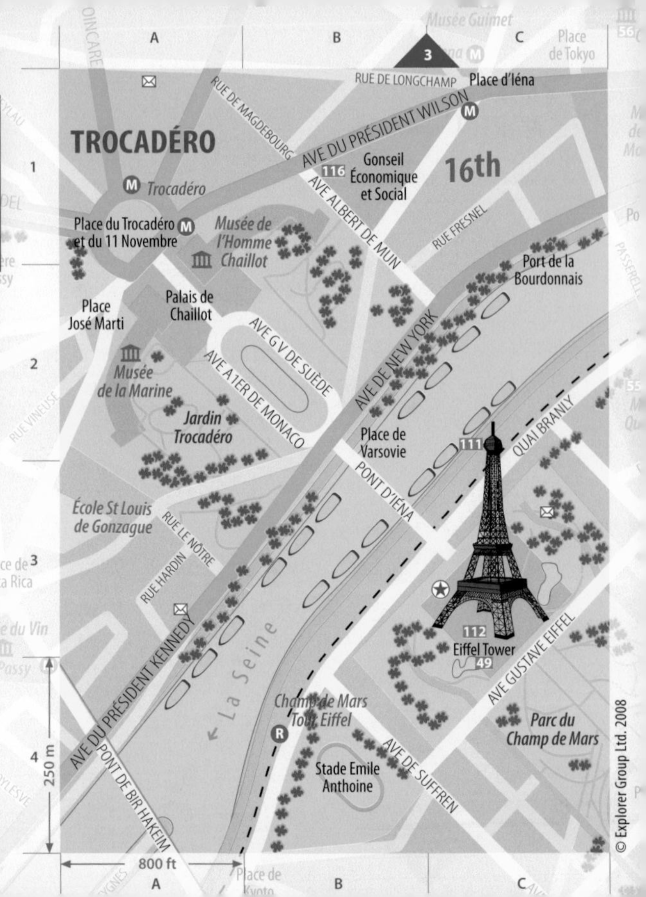

© Explorer Group Ltd. 2008

250 m

800 ft

Place de
Kyoto

A   B   C

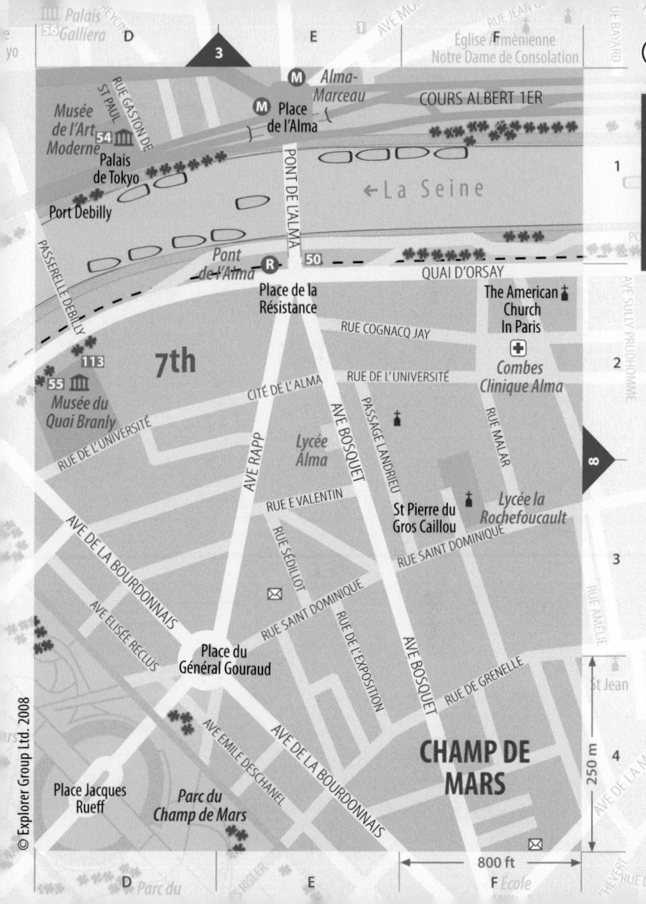

Map 7

D

Palais
Galliera

Éslise F'rménienne
Notre Dame de Consolation

N

3

E

AVE M

RUE JEAN

LE BAYARD

RUE FRANÇOIS

yo

RUE GASTON DE

ST PAUL

M Alma-
Marceau

M Place
de l'Alma

COURS ALBERT 1ER

Musée
de l'Art
Moderne

54 Palais
de Tokyo

PONT DE L'ALMA

← La Seine

1

Port Debilly

PASSERELLE DEBILLY

Pont
de l'Alma

R

50

QUAI D'ORSAY

Place de la
Résistance

RUE COGNACQ JAY

The American
Church
In Paris

AVE SULLY PRUDHOMME

7th

RUE DE L'UNIVERSITÉ

CITÉ DE L'ALMA

RUE DE L'UNIVERSITÉ

Combes
Clinique Alma

2

113

55 Musée du
Quai Branly

PASSAGE LANDRIEU

RUE MALAR

8

Lycée
Álma

AVE RAPP

AVE BOSQUET

RUE E VALENTIN

St Pierre du
Gros Caillou

Lycée la
Rochefoucault

RUE SÉDILLOT

RUE SAINT DOMINIQUE

RUE SAINT DOMINIQUE

3

AVE DE LA BOURDONNAIS

AVE ELISÉE RECLUS

Place du
Général Gouraud

RUE DE L'EXPOSITION

AVE BOSQUET

RUE DE GRENELLE

St Jean

RUE AMÉLIE

250 m

Place Jacques
Rueff

AVE EMILE DESCHANEL

Parc du
Champ de Mars

AVE DE LA BOURDONNAIS

**CHAMP DE
MARS**

4

RUE DE LA MOTTE PIC

© Explorer Group Ltd. 2008

800 ft

289

D

Parc du

E

F

École

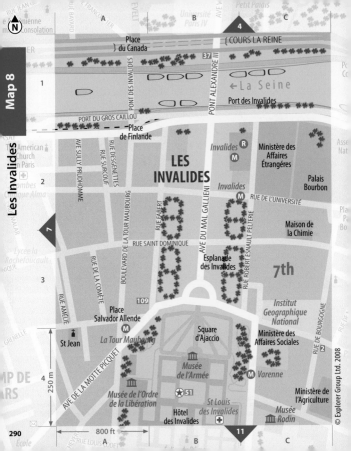

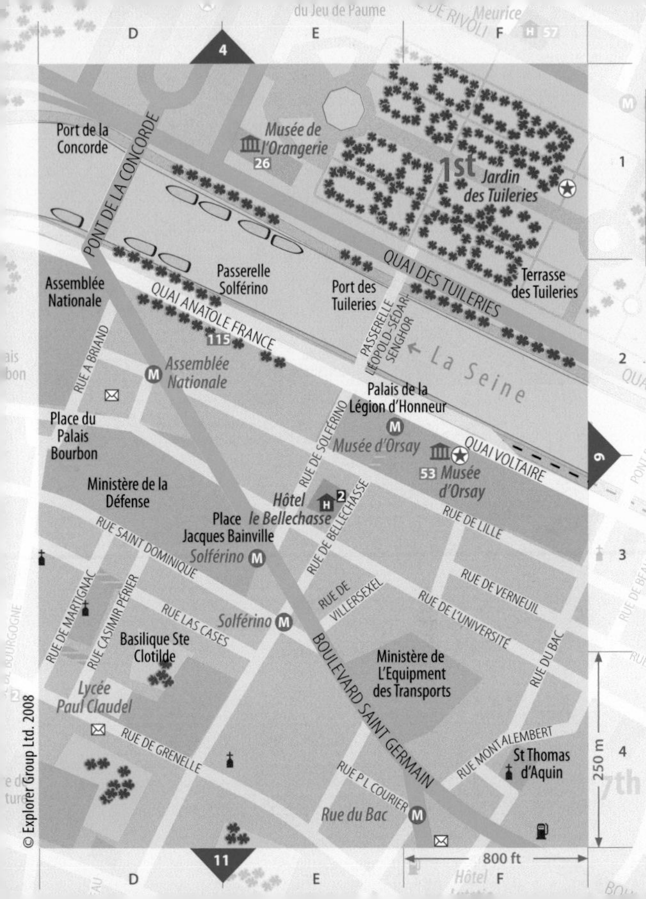

Map 8

du Jeu de Paume

Meurice

DE RIVOLI

H 57

N

D 4 E F

Port de la Concorde

Musée de l'Orangerie 26

1st

Jardin des Tuileries

PONT DE LA CONCORDE

1

Assemblée Nationale

Passerelle Solférino

QUAI ANATOLE FRANCE

Port des Tuileries

QUAI DES TUILERIES

Terrasse des Tuileries

PASSERELLE LEOPOLD SEDAR SENGHOR

La Seine

QUAI FR

2

RUE A BRIAND

Assemblée Nationale

Palais de la Légion d'Honneur

9

PONT ROYAL

Place du Palais Bourbon

RUE DE SOLFERINO

Musée d'Orsay

QUAI VOLTAIRE

Musée d'Orsay 53

Ministère de la Défense

Hôtel le Bellechasse 2

RUE DE LILLE

RUE SAINT DOMINIQUE

Place Jacques Bainville

Solférino

RUE DE BELLECHASSE

RUE DE VERNEUIL

RUE DE BEAUNE

3

RUE DE MARTIGNAC

RUE CASIMIR PERIER

Solférino

RUE LAS CASES

RUE DE VILLERSEXEL

RUE DE L'UNIVERSITÉ

RUE DE VERNE

Basilique Ste Clotilde

Ministère de L'Equipement des Transports

RUE DU BAC

Lycée Paul Claudel

BOULEVARD SAINT GERMAIN

RUE DE GRENELLE

RUE MONT ALEMBERT

St Thomas d'Aquin

250 m

4

RUE PL COURIER

7th

Rue du Bac

© Explorer Group Ltd. 2008

11

D E

800 ft

F

291

Hôtel

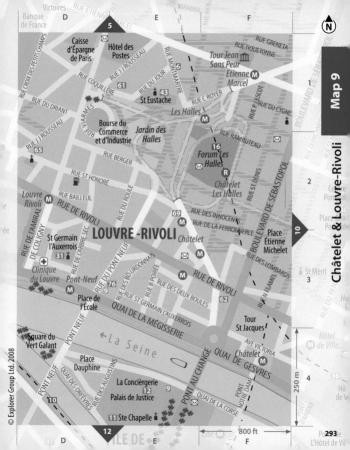

Map 9

Map 10

N

St Nicolas des
Champs

RUE DE TURBIGO

BEAUBOURG

Square du
Temple

3rd

RUE AU MAIRE

RUE DES GRAVILLIERS

RUE CHAPON

RUE DE MONTMORENCY

BOULEVARD DE SÉBASTOPOL

RUE DU BOURG L'ABBÉ

RUE AUX OURS

RUE QUINCAMPOIX

RUE ST MARTIN

RUE BEAUBOURG

RUE MICHEL LE COMTE

Musée de
la Poupée

Musée d'Art
et d'Histoire
du Judaïsme

RUE DU TEMPLE

RUE DES ARCHIVES

RUE PASTOURELLE

Musée de la
Chasse et
de la Nature

RUE PORTEFOIN

Galerie
Marian
Goodman

Archives
Nationales

Musée de
l'Histoire
de France

RUE DES QUATRE-FILS

Cathédrale
Ste Croix

Centre
Pompidou

Place Georges
Pompidou

RUE RAMBUTEAU

RUE DES FRANCS BOURGEOIS

Hôtel
de Rohan

RUE BARBETTE

Place
Étienne
Michelet

St Merri

RUE DU RENARD

RUE SIMON LE FRANC

RUE DU PLÂTRE

RUE DES BLANCS MANTEAUX

Hôtel Duo

Clinique
du Sport
du Marais

Tour
St Jacques

AVE VICTORIA

Châtelet

Billettes

RUE DE MOUSSY

RUE AUBRIOT

RUE VIEILLE DU TEMPLE

Hôtel
de Ville

BHV

Hôtel
de Ville

Hôtel
Caron
de Beaumarchais

RUE DES ROSIERS

RUE DU ROI DE SICILE

RUE FERDINAND DUVAL

Centre
Malher

Hôtel
de Ville

RUE DE RIVOLI

PONT D'ARCOLE

Porte de
L'Hôtel de Ville

RUE FRANÇOIS MIRON

St Paul

4th

Beaubourg & The Marais

250 m

800 ft

4 m

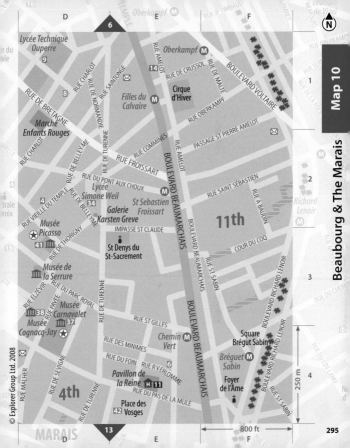

Map 11

South Of Invalides

© Explorer Group Ltd. 2008

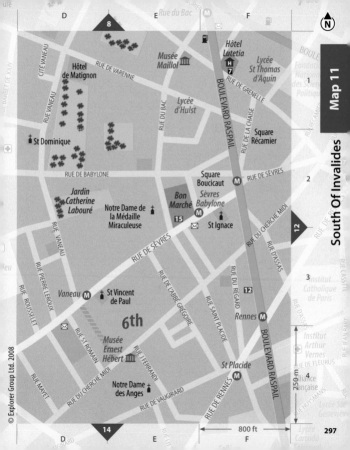

Map 11

South Of Invalides

N

D · E · Rue du Bac · M · F

8

CITÉ VANEAU

Rue du Bac

Hôtel
Lutetia

H 7

Musée
Maillol

Lycée
St Thomas
d'Aquin

RUE DE VARENNE

Hôtel
de Matignon

Rue de Grenelle

1

RUE VANEAU

BOULEVARD RASPAIL

RUE DE LA CHAISE

Lycée
d'Hulst

Rue du Bac

Square
Récamier

St Dominique

RUE DE BABYLONE

RUE DE SÈVRES

2

M

Square
Boucicaut

Jardin
Catherine
Labouré

Bon
Marché

Sèvres
Babylone

RUE DU CHERCHE MIDI

12

Notre Dame de
la Médaille
Miraculeuse

15

M

St Ignace

RUE VANEAU

RUE DE SÈVRES

RUE D'ASSAS

RUE PIERRE LEROUX

RUE DE L'ABBÉ GRÉGOIRE

3

Institut
Catholique
de Paris

Vaneau

M

St Vincent
de Paul

12

RUE DU REGARD

RUE DE ROUSSELET

6th

Rennes

M

RUE SAINT PLACIDE

Institut
Arthur
Vernes

Musée
Ernest
Hébert

RUE ST ROMAIN

RUE J FERRANDI

RUE DE FLEURUS

RUE MAYET

RUE DU CHERCHE MIDI

Notre Dame
des Anges

RUE DE VAUGIRARD

St Placide

M

4

RUE DE RENNES

BOULEVARD RASPAIL

250 m

14

D · E · 800 ft · F

297

© Explorer Group Ltd. 2008

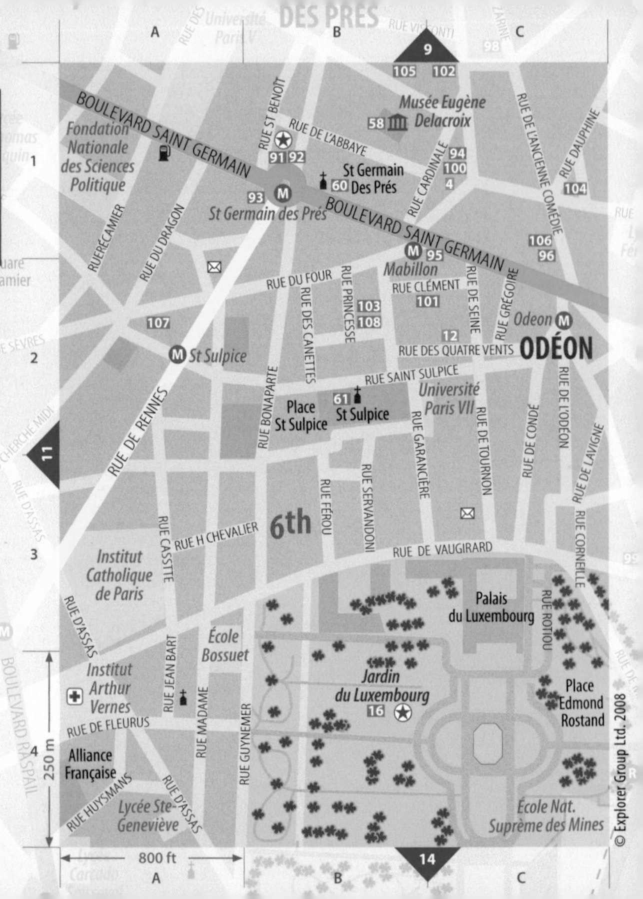

RUE DES Université Paris V RUE VISCONTI ZABRIE

DES PRÉS

9
105 102
98

C

Map 12

BOULEVARD SAINT GERMAIN

Fondation Nationale des Sciences Politique

RUE ST BENOÎT

RUE ST BENOÎT

RUE DE L'ABBAYE

Musée Eugène Delacroix
58

RUE CARDINALE

RUE DE L'ANCIENNE COMÉDIE

RUE DE DAUPHINE

104

91 92

St Germain Des Prés
60

94
100
4

RUE DE SEINE

106
96

RUE GRÉGOIRE

93

St Germain des Prés

BOULEVARD SAINT GERMAIN

95

Mabillon

RUE CLÉMENT

101

RUE PRINCESSE

RUE DES CANETTES

RUE DU FOUR

103
108

12

RUE DES QUATRE VENTS

ODÉON

Odeon

RUE DE L'ODÉON

107

St Sulpice

RUE BONAPARTE

RUE SAINT SULPICE

61
St Sulpice

Université Paris VII

RUE DE CONDÉ

RUE DE L'ODÉON

RUE DE LAVIGNE

RUE DE RENNES

Place St Sulpice

RUE GARANCIÈRE

RUE DE TOURNON

RUE DE SEVRES

RUE DU CHERCHE MIDI

6th

RUE FÉROU

RUE SERVANDONI

RUE DE VAUGIRARD

RUE CORNEILLE

RUE CASSETTE

RUE H CHEVALIER

Institut Catholique de Paris

RUE D'ASSAS

Institut Arthur Vernes

RUE JEAN BART

École Bossuet

RUE MADAME

RUE GUYNEMER

Palais du Luxembourg

RUE ROTROU

RUE DE FLEURUS

Jardin du Luxembourg
16

Place Edmond Rostand

Alliance Française

BOULEVARD RASPAIL

RUE D'ASSAS

RUE HUYSMANS

Lycée Ste Geneviève

École Nat. Suprême des Mines

14

© Explorer Group Ltd. 2008

800 ft
250 m

A B C

11

Map 12

Odéon & The Latin Quarter

N

9

Ste Chapelle

Palais de Justice

ÎLE DE LA CITÉ

Cité

Préfecture de Police

Hôtel Dieu

Porte de l'Hô...

QUAI AUX FLEURS

1

RUE DE SAVOIE

97

RUE SÉGUIER

PONT ST MICHEL

St Michel

QUAI DU MARCHÉ NEUF

St Michel Notre Dame

10

Place du Parvis Notre Dame

13

RUE D'ARCOLE

RUE DE LA CITÉ

RUE ST ANDRÉ DES ARTS

Lycée Fénelon

RUE SUGER

St Michel

RUE GIT LE COEUR

RUE DE LA HUCHETTE

PETIT PONT

St Michel Notre Dame

PONT AU DOUBLE

Cathédrale Notre Dame

8

RUE MIGNON

RUE HAUTEFEUILLE

St-Séverin

22

RUE GALANDE

52

QUAI DE MONTEBELLO

2

Université Paris Descartes

3

RUE P SARRAZIN

Cluny la Sorbonne

BOULEVARD SAINT GERMAIN

RUE DANTE

55

RUE DE BIÈVRE

Maubert Mutualité

Place Maubert

13

Musée de l'Assistance Publ

RUE RACINE

Musée National du Moyen Age, Thermes de Cluny

20

5th

RUE DU SOMMERARD

RUE DES CARMES

Hôtel Abba Saint Germ

St Nicolas Chardo

Lycée St Louis

RUE DE LA SORBONNE

Université Paris IV

Sorbonne

Collège de France

RUE DES CARMES

RUE MONGE

Palais de Mutualité

H

99

BOULEVARD SAINT MICHEL

RUE MONSIEUR LE PRINCE

LATIN QUARTER

RUE JEAN DE BEAUVAIS

St Ephrem

56

RUE DES ÉCOLES

43

RUE DE MÉDICIS

Lycée J Monod

RUE LE GOFF

RUE TOULLIER

Lycée Louis le Grand

Collège Ste Barbe

RUE LAPLACE

Square Paul Langevin

Jardin Carré

RUE DESCARTES

Cardinal Lemoine

250 m

RUE SAINT-JACQUES

Université Paris I Panthéon Sorbonne

RUE CUJAS

57

RUE DU CARDINAL LEMOINE

4

Luxembourg

RUE ROYER COLLARD

48

Le Panthéon

18

RUE CLOTILDE

St Étienne du Mont

RUE CLOVIS

© Explorer Group Ltd 2008

15

D

E

Lycée Henri IV

800 ft

F

Map 13

(N)

RUE DE VILLE

RUE FRANÇO...

...E. RIVOLI

Malhen

A

B

10

C

M St Paul

Porte de
L'Hôtel de Ville

QUAI AUX FLEURS

QUAI DE L'HÔTEL DE VILLE

RUE DE L'HÔTEL DEVILLE

4th

Lycée
St German

RUE DE JOU...

M

Lycée
Charlemagne

PONT LOUIS PHILIPPE

QUAI DE BOURBON

RUE DES NONNAINS DHYÈRES

Hôtel
de Sens

RUE DE L'AVE MARIA

Hôtel
...ieu

QUAI AUX FLEURS

1

Cathédrale
Notre Dame

13

QUAI DE L'ARCHEVÊCHÉ

PONT
ST LOUIS

ÎLE SAINT
LOUIS

44

RUE LE REGRATTIER

RUE BUDÉ

Pont Marie

PONT
MARIE

QUAI DES CÉLESTINS

Porte
des Célestins

RUE SAINT LOUIS EN L'ÎLE

8 St Louis

40

QUAI D'ANJOU

Hôtel de
Lauzun

H

Hôtel
Lambert

RUE DES DEUX PONTS

La Seine

QUAI D'ORLÉANS

QUAI DE BÉTHUNE

PONT DE L'ARCHEVÊCHÉ

2

Pont de
l'Archevêché

RUE DE BIÈVRE

MONTEBELLO

Place
...bert

12

Musée de
l'Assistance
Publique

PONT DE LA TOURNELLE

PONT DE SULLY

42

Hôtel Abbatial
Saint Germain

H St Nicolas du
Chardonnet

Place
Mohammed V

41 19

RUE DE POISSY

3

Palais de la
Mutualité

Institut
du Monde Arabe

QUAI SAINT BERNARD

RUE DES ÉCOLES

45

119

43

RUE DES FOSSÉS SAINT BERNARD

RUE MONGE

...em

Square Paul
Langevin

Jardin
Carré

Cardinal
Lemoine

Musée de
Minéralogie

Faculté des
Sciences

RUE DES ARÈNES

250 m

M

Cardinal Lemoine

RUE DU CARDINAL LEMOINE

5th

Place
Jussieu

RUE CUVIER

RUE CLOVIS

4

RUE DES...

...nne
...ont

800 ft

M Jussieu

© Explorer Group Ltd. 2008

A

Arènes
de Lutèce

B

15

C

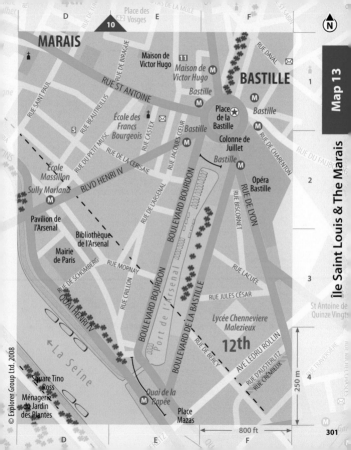

Map 13

N

D · E · F

Place des Vosges

10

RUE DE LA MULE

RUE SAINT-GILLES

RUE DE BIRAGUE

MARAIS

Maison de Victor Hugo

11 Maison de Victor Hugo

RUE DAVAL

BASTILLE

RUE ST ANTOINE

M Bastille

M Bastille

RUE SABIN

RUE DE BEAUTREILLIS

RUE SAINT PAUL

École des Francs Bourgeois

RUE CASTEX

RUE JACQUES CŒUR

M Bastille

Place de la Bastille

★ Colonne de Juillet

M Bastille

M Bastille

RUE DE CHARENTON

RUE DU FAUBOURG

RUE DU PETIT MUSC

RUE DE LA CERISAIE

M Bastille

Opéra Bastille

RUE DE LYON

RUE BISCORNET

École Massillon

BLVD HENRI IV

RUE DE L'ARSENAL

BOULEVARD BOURDON

M Sully Morland

Pavilion de l'Arsenal

Bibliothèque de l'Arsenal

RUE CRILLON

RUE MORNAY

RUE LACUÉE

RUE DE SCHOMBERG

Port de l'Arsenal

RUE JULES CÉSAR

Mairie de Paris

BOULEVARD BOURDON

BOULEVARD DE LA BASTILLE

RUE DE BERCY

12th

QUAI HENRI IV

Lycée Chenneviere Malezieux

AVE LEDRU ROLLIN

St Antoine de Quinze Vingts

← La Seine

RUE D'AUSTERLITZ

RUE CRÉMIEUX

RUE TRAVERSIÈRE

Square Tino Rossi

Ménagerie du Jardin des Plantes

Quai de la Rapée

M

Place Mazas

M

250 m

800 ft

1 · 2 · 3 · 4

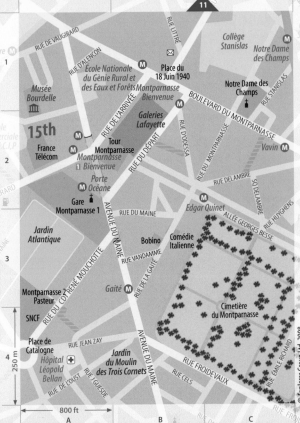

Map 14

Montparnasse

RUE DE VAUGIRARD

RUE LITTRÉ

Collège
Stanislas

Notre Dame
des Champs

RUE D'ALENÇON

Musée
Bourdelle

École Nationale
du Gènie Rural et
des Eaux et Forêts

Place du
18 Juin 1940

Montparnasse
Bienvenue

Notre Dame des
Champs

BOULEVARD DU MONTPARNASSE

RUE STANISLAS

RUE DE VAUGIRARD

École
Commerciale
de la C.C.I.P.

15th

France
Télécom

Galeries
Lafayette

RUE D'ODESSA

Vavin

RUE DE L'ARRIVÉE

Tour
Montparnasse

Montparnasse
Bienvenue

RUE DU DÉPART

RUE DU MONTPARNASSE

RUE DELAMBRE

BD DELAMBRE

RUE HUYGHENS

Porte
Océane

Gare
Montparnasse 1

AVENUE DU MAINE

RUE DU MAINE

Edgar Quinet

ALLÉE GEORGES BESSE

Jardin
Atlantique

Bobino

RUE VANDAMME

Comédie
Italienne

RUE DE LA GAÎTÉ

Montparnasse 2
Pasteur

RUE DU CDT RENÉ MOUCHOTTE

Gaîté

SNCF

Cimetière
du Montparnasse

Place de
Catalogne

RUE JEAN ZAY

AVENUE DU MAINE

RUE FROIDEVAUX

RUE ÉMILE RICHARD

Hôpital
Léopold
Bellan

Jardin
du Moulin
des Trois Cornets

RUE DE L'OUEST

RUE J GUESDE

RUE CELS

RUE DAGUERRE

ALLÉE DU CAPITAINE DRONNE

BD MONTPARNASSE VAUGIRARD

© Explorer Group Ltd. 2008

250 m

800 ft

A   B   C

Map 14

12

N

Lycée
Carcado
Saisseval

RUE HUYSMANS

RUE D'ASSAS

Ste
Geneviève

École Nat.
Supreme des Mines

RUE JEAN Cv

D **E** **F**

RUE VAVIN

Lycée
de Sion

6th

RUE BRÉA

RUE AUGUSTE COMTE

Lycée
Montaigne

Luxembourg **R**

Jardin
Marco Polo
Place E Denis

1

St J
du H

Institu
Natl
de Jeunes
Sourds

Université
Paris II

Musée Zadkine
59 🏛

RUE D'ASSAS

Université
Paris V

Observatoire

RUE MICHELET

Jardin Robert
Cavalier de la
Salle

Lycée
Lavoisier

2

MONTPARNASSE

RUE JOSEPH BARA

RUE LE VERRIER

École
Alsacienne

Tarnier ✚

Place E Denis

St Marcel ♱

BOULEVARD SAINT MICHEL

Lycée
Sevigné

15

RUE HENRI BARBUSSE

RUE NOTRE DAME des CHAMPS

BOULEVARD DU MONTPARNASSE

✉

RUE P NICOLE

RUE SAINT JACQUES

Lycée
Paul Bert

Raspail **M**

RUE CAMPAGNE PREMIÈRE

✝

Port
Royal **R**

3

PORT ROYAL

14th

RUE BOISSONADE

Maternité ✚
Clinique

BOULEVARD RASPAIL

École Speciale
d'Architecture

Fondation
Cartier

Hôpital St
Vincent de Paul ✚

Port Royal
Baudelocque

RUE CASSINI

RUE DU FAUBOURG SAINT JACQUES

250 m

✚

4

AVENUE DE L'OBSERVATOIRE

AVE DENFERT ROCHEREAU

♱ Tour Les Saints

Observatoire
de Paris

800 ft

RUE MÉCH

RUE FROIDEVAUX

Aéroports
de Paris

D **E** **F**

Map 15

Le Panthéon
18
St Étienne
du Mont
RUE CLOVIS
12

RUE ROYER COLLARD

RUE DE L'ESTRAPADE

Lycée
Henri IV

RUE THOUIN

RUE PIERRE ET MARIE CURIE

RUE BLAINVILLE

Place de la
Contrescarpe

St Jacques
du Haut Pas

Institut Oceanique
Centre de la Mer

Marché
Mouffetard
11

L'Adoration

Institut
de Recherche
Pédagogique

54

Institut
National
de Jeunes
Sourds

Hôpital Claudius
Regaud

RUE DU POT DE FER

RUE ERASME BROSSOLETTE

Lycée
Lavoisier

RUE DES URSULINES

École Normale
Supérieure

Maison
Fraternelle

Place Alfred
Kastler

RUE J CALVIN

École Supérieure
de Physique

5th

RUE L'HOMOND

RUE DES FEUILLANTINES

RUE VAUQUELIN

RUE SAINT JACQUES

St Médard

Institut Nat
Agronomique

RUE BERTHOLLET

RUE DE L'ARBALÈTE

RUE CLAUDE BERNARD

Val de Grâce

Institut de
l'Administration
des Entreprises [IAE]

RUE DES LYONNAIS

BOULEVARD DE PORT ROYAL

250 m

Cochin

RUE BERTHOLLET

RUE BROCA

RUE PASCAL

Port Royal

RUE SAINT HIPPOLYTE

304

RUE MÉCHAIN

800 ft

BOULEVARD ARAGO

© Explorer Group Ltd. 2008

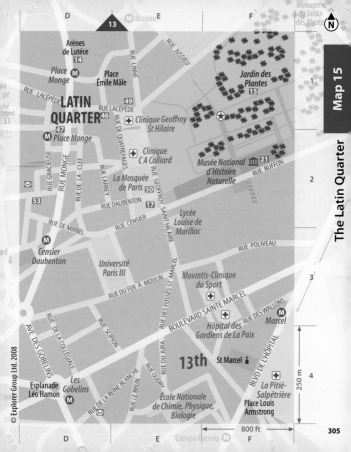

Map 15

13

Menagerie
du Jardin
des Plantes

N

Arènes
de Lutéce
14

Place
Monge

Place
Émile Mâle

RUE LINNÉ

RUE JUSSIEU

Jardin des
Plantes
15

RUE LACÉPÈDE

LATIN
QUARTER
46

49

RUE LACÉPÈDE

47 Place Monge

RUE DE QUATREFAGES

Clinique Geoffroy
St Hilaire

Clinique
C A Colliard

RUE GRACIEUSE

RUE MONGE

RUE DE LA CLEF

RUE LARREY

La Mosquée
de Paris 50

17

RUE GEOFFROY SAINT HILAIRE

Musée National
d'Histoire
Naturelle

21

RUE BUFFON

53

RUE DAUBENTON

RUE DE MIRBEL

RUE CENSIER

Lycée
Louise de
Marillac

Censier
Daubenton

Université
Paris III

RUE DU FER À MOULIN

RUE POLIVEAU

Movintis-Clinique
du Sport

RUE DES FOSSÉS ST MARCEL

BOULEVARD SAINTE MARCEL

RUE DES WALLONS

Marcel

AVE DES GOBELINS

RUE DE LA COLLÉGIALE

RUE SCIPION

RUE DU JURA

Hôpital des
Gardiens de La Paix

13th

St Marcel

BLVD DE L'HÔPITAL

La Pitié-
Salpêtrière

Esplanade
Léo Hamon

Les
Gobelins

RUE DE LA REINE BLANCHE

RUE LE BRUN

RUE OUDRY

École Nationale
de Chimie, Physique,
Biologie

Place Louis
Armstrong

250 m

800 ft

Campo Formio

© Explorer Group Ltd. 2008